Better Homes and Gardens®

QUICK & EASY
WOODCRAFTS

© Copyright 1987 by Meredith Corporation, Des Moines, Iowa.
All Rights Reserved. Printed in the United States of America.
First Edition. Fourth Printing, 1988.
Library of Congress Catalog Card Number: 86-62168
ISBN: 0-696-02610-9 (hard cover)
ISBN: 0-696-01611-7 (trade paperback)

BETTER HOMES AND GARDENS® BOOKS

Editor: Gerald M. Knox
Art Director: Ernest Shelton
Managing Editor: David A. Kirchner
Editorial Project Managers: James D. Blume,
    Marsha Jahns, Rosanne Weber Mattson,
    Mary Helen Schiltz

Senior Crafts Books Editor: Joan Cravens
Associate Crafts Books Editors: Liz Porter,
    Beverly Rivers, Sara Jane Treinen

Associate Art Directors: Linda Ford Vermie,
    Neoma Alt West, Randall Yontz
Assistant Art Directors: Lynda Haupert,
    Harijs Priekulis, Tom Wegner
Senior Graphic Designers: Stan Sams,
    Darla Whipple-Frain
Graphic Designers: Mike Burns, Brian Wignall
Art Production: Director, John Berg;
    Associate, Joe Heuer;
    Office Manager, Emma Rediger

President, Book Group: Fred Stines
Vice President, General Manager: Jeramy Lanigan
Vice President, Retail Marketing: Jamie Martin
Vice President, Administrative Services: Rick Rundall

BETTER HOMES AND GARDENS® MAGAZINE
President, Magazine Group: James A. Autry
Vice President, Editorial Director: Doris Eby
Executive Director, Editorial Services: Duane L. Gregg

MEREDITH CORPORATE OFFICERS
Chairman of the Board: E.T. Meredith III
President: Robert A. Burnett
Executive Vice President: Jack D. Rehm

QUICK AND EASY WOODCRAFTS
Crafts Editor: Sara Jane Treinen
Contributing Editor: Michael Stowers
Editorial Project Manager: Rosanne Weber Mattson
Graphic Designer: Stan Sams
Electronic Text Processor: Paula Forest

Cover project: See page 7.

CONTENTS

YARD AND DECK TRIMS

FOR OUTDOOR FUN

Want to make your yard the cat's meow? Then craft these whimsical house numbers, or any of the practical and decorative items in this chapter, to personalize your garden and enhance your family's enjoyment. Wooden outdoor trims, painted or finished naturally, bring warmth and individuality to any home.

If you're a cat fancier, let the cat family, *opposite,* be the first to greet your family and friends.

Mother cat bears your family name, while all her kittens display your house numbers. Each cat sits atop a pressure-treated wood stake that is fancifully painted. The cats and flowers are cut from tempered hardboard that will endure any weather, because all the parts are painted with outdoor latex paints.

Make just enough kittens, stakes, and flowers for your street address.

You easily can adapt this same design to fit a canine member of your household. Sketch a simple outline drawing of the shape of your dog, or look through your children's coloring books to find a pattern for a dog that looks like yours.

Instructions for the projects in this chapter begin on page 10.

YARD AND DECK TRIMS

Scraps of lumber supply the makings for the bird-pleasing projects on these two pages. Make one or all of them and you'll enjoy watching the comings and goings of your feathered friends all year long.

The brightly painted apple house with its worm perch, *above,* will attract nesting birds in the early spring. Full-size patterns for the apple, worm, and leaf motifs make this project easy and quick to build.

On cold winter days, feed suet to your backyard birds using the cardinal and goldfinch suet feeders, *opposite.*

Birds love suet, and they need it, especially in winter, to maintain their healthy feathered bodies. To keep your yard birds happy and nourished, roll birdseed into lard, then shape the mixture into a ball. Center the ball in the opening of the feeder, using the wire insert to stabilize it.

YARD AND DECK TRIMS

Liven up your garden beds with the squirrel or rabbit planter boxes, *opposite*. These larger-than-life critters stand 18 inches tall and are 21¼ inches long. Filled with geraniums, marigolds, petunias, or any of your favorite flowers, they can be moved around your garden to add touches of color until other flowers begin to bloom.

Build them from redwood or exterior plywood to withstand the elements. Then woodburn their body outlines and facial details. Refer to page 67 for helpful hints for woodburning.

For those gardeners who specialize in growing herbs, the table planter, *above*, presents a splendid way to grow your favorite herbs—basil, parsley, chives—and it keeps them accessible.

The table stands 22¼ inches high and is 48 inches long. Five 6-inch-diameter holes are cut from the center of the table to hold the planted clay pots.

When you entertain on your patio or deck, temporarily remove the pots and replace them with baskets, plates, or clay pots filled with party treats.

YARD AND DECK TRIMS

Cat Family House Numbers

Shown on pages 4–5.

Design is approximately 38 inches wide and about 18 inches tall (from tips of stakes to tops of small cats) before being placed into the ground.

MATERIALS

Five 2-foot lengths of pressure-treated 1x3s for stakes
Scraps of ¼-inch tempered hardboard for cats and flowers
Four 11-inch strips of ¼x1½-inch lattice
Oil-base primer
Red, green, gray, white, and black outdoor latex paints
Ten 1-inch No. 5 wood screws
Finishing nails
Scrap of plywood, approximately 10x30 inches, for brace

INSTRUCTIONS

Note: The materials list and instructions are for a house number with four numbers. Adjust the number of stakes, small cats, and lattice strips to accommodate your own family house numbers.

Trace, then transfer, the full-size pattern for the large cat on pages 12 and 13 onto the tempered hardboard. *Note:* To complete the large cat, align the A-B dashed line on the right side of the cat on page 12 with the A-B dashed line on the pattern on top of page 13; cut out.

Trace, then transfer, the full-size pattern for the small cat on page 11 onto the hardboard; cut out four small cats.

Bore a ½-inch hole in *each* of the tail cutouts, then insert your saw blade into the holes to complete the cutouts.

Trace, then transfer, the flower pattern on page 12 onto the hardboard and cut out 5 flowers.

Cut points on one end of each 2-foot stake for easy insertion into the ground.

Lightly sand and prime all the pieces. Using the photo on pages 4 and 5 as a guide, paint the cats, flowers, and stakes. Paint your family name atop the large cat and your house numbers atop the remaining cats.

Center the cats on the stakes so the top of the stake is even with the tail cutout for the small cats and 2 inches below the cutout of the large cat. Then attach the cats with glue and finishing nails. Set the nails with a light tap or two with your hammer. Fill the holes with wood putty; let dry, then sand smooth. Touch up painting.

When paint is dry, position the cat stakes on the 10x30-inch plywood scrap. This plywood piece braces the cats until you get them into the ground. The stakes for the small cats are 5 inches apart and the stake for the large cat is 6 inches from the stake to its left. Check to be sure the bottoms of the cat figures are on an even line. Screw through the back side of the plywood into each stake with two 1-inch No. 5 wood screws. Then place the lattice pieces atop the stakes as shown in the drawing, *below,* starting 1½ inches from the cat on the left. Cut miters in the lattice pieces by marking directly from their placement. Attach lattice pieces with finishing nails and a dab of glue. Attach the flowers in the same manner. Touch up any damaged painting.

In the yard, lay the assembly on the grass with the points on the spots where you want the assembly to stand. At one end point, drive a stake in the ground to a depth of 6 inches. Wiggle the stake a little and then pull it out and drive it in the ground at the next point. Repeat this step for all 5 points. Then set the sign in the ground and tamp the soil to hold the sign in place.

Remove the plywood brace, fill the screw holes, and touch up any damaged paint.

Apple Bird House

Shown on page 6.

The finished house is 7¾ inches wide, 8 inches high, and 7½ inches from front to back.

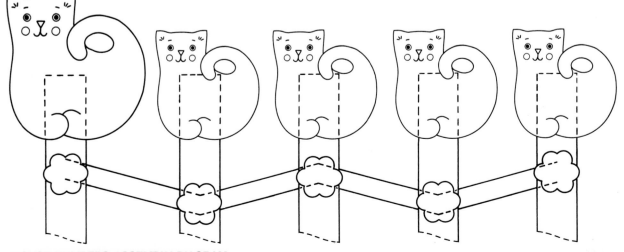

HOUSE NUMBERS ASSEMBLY DIAGRAM

MATERIALS

Scraps of ¾-inch fir or pine
Scrap of ¼-inch hardboard for
  leaves
Scrap of ⅜-inch lattice for perch
Wood primer
Red, green, brown, and yellow
  oil-base paints
Glue; 4d finishing nails

INSTRUCTIONS

Trace and transfer the full-size patterns on page 13 for the apple to the scrap fir and for the leaf to the ¼-inch hardboard. Cut out 2 apple and leaf parts. Bore the holes in the *front* apple piece for the bird's entrance and the worm perch. Transfer pattern for worm to lattice or fir trim. Use a coping saw to cut out the worm if your scrap piece is not very big. Secure the worm piece in a vise while cutting.

Mark out the center pieces (roof, sides, and floor) on ¾-inch scraps. Mark a full 2 inches extra (this is called overwidth), and be sure to keep the grain going the same way—from front to back.

Cut all these pieces 6 inches long; cut widths following the dimensions on the drawing. Mark, then cut the bevels.

For ease of assembly, mount one piece in a vise or clamp. Join roof pieces with finishing nails and glue.

Let the glue in the roof assembly dry while you join the two side pieces to the floor, again using finishing nails and glue. When glue is dry in all parts, join the side/floor assembly to the roof assembly. Position the apple parts according to the drawing and attach with nails and glue.

Sand and prime the house, leaves, and perch. Paint front and back red; paint roof, sides, and floor green. For ease in painting, paint leaves and perch separately and then glue to house when paint is dry.

SMALL CAT
Cut 4

HOUSE NUMBERS

FLOWER
Cut 5

A

LARGE CAT
Cut 1

B

HOUSE NUMBERS

YARD AND DECK TRIMS

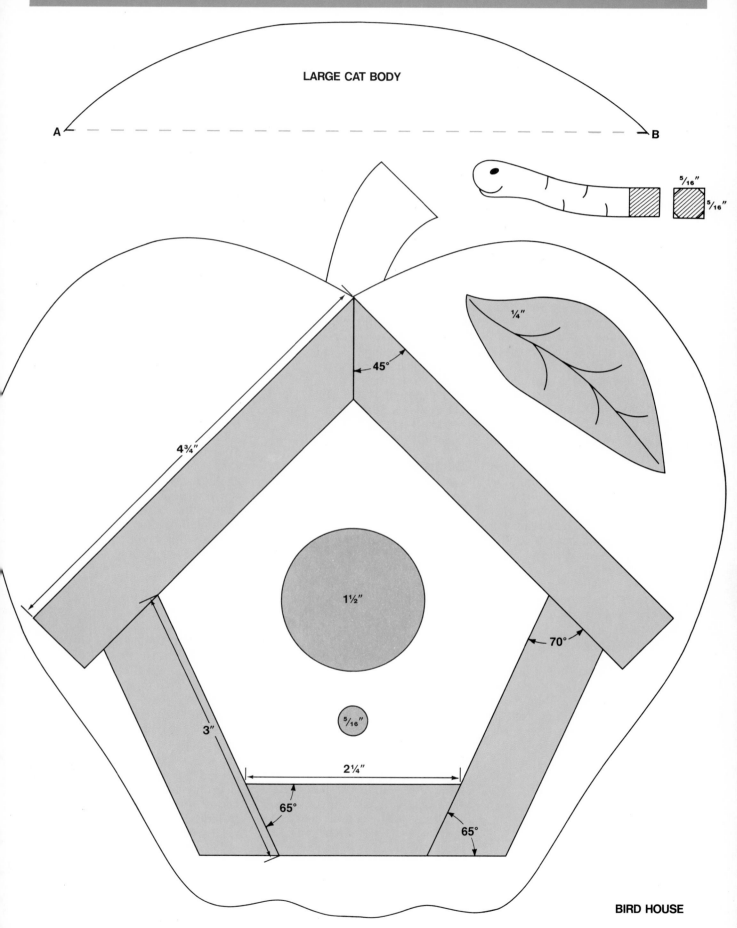

LARGE CAT BODY

A — B

5/16″

5/16″

1/4″

45°

4 3/4″

1 1/2″

70°

5/16″

3″

2 1/4″

65°

65°

BIRD HOUSE

YARD AND DECK TRIMS

Bird Suet Feeders

Shown on page 7.

Cardinal is 7¼x8 inches; goldfinch is 6⅛x9 inches.

MATERIALS
Scraps of ¾-inch fir or pine
Red, orange, black, and white
    acrylic paints for cardinal
Yellow, black, orange, and white
    acrylic paints for goldfinch
Exterior varnish
6-inch length of coat hanger
    wire to hold suet for *each*
    feeder
1 small screw eye for hanger
Length of light-gauge wire
    (rustproof) for hanging
Suet seed cake (available at
    garden centers or pet stores)

INSTRUCTIONS
    Select bird pattern, pages 16
and 17, of your choice. Trace the
full-size pattern onto tracing paper and transfer markings onto
fir; cut shape from wood. Cut out
center hole. For placement of wire
to hold the suet, use a ⅛-inch bit
and bore a hole through the top of
bird's back and ⅛-inch deep into
the bottom section (see diagram
on page 16 for placement). Lightly sand the shaped piece.
    Trace the painting lines onto
both sides of the feeder, then
paint, using the photo on page 6
as a guide. Allow paint to dry; coat
with varnish.
    With needlenose pliers, form a
small loop at one end of the coat
hanger wire. Remove a handful of
suet from its container and shape
into ball about the size of a baseball and place in the center of the
bird opening. Insert the coat
hanger wire through the top hole,
through the suet cake, and anchor it in the hole at base of bird.
    Fasten the screw eye and attach
the light-gauge wire to hang.

Animal Planters

Shown on page 8.

Planters are approximately 21½
inches long and 18 inches high.

MATERIALS
For the rabbit
80 inches of ¾x10-inch
    redwood for the end pieces
40 inches of ¾x8-inch redwood
    for the box sides
20 inches of ¾x6-inch redwood
    for the box floor
For the squirrel
80 inches of ¾x10-inch
    redwood for the end pieces
40 inches of ¾x10-inch
    redwood for the box sides
20 inches of ¾x6-inch redwood
    for the box floor
For both planters
Waterproof glue
Finishing nails
1¼-inch No. 6 countersink wood
    screws
Woodburning tool

INSTRUCTIONS
    Note: Planters are built from
redwood, but you can easily substitute pressure-treated plywood.
    Cut box parts as follows: *For
the squirrel,* cut two side pieces
measuring 8½x20 inches. Cut
two end pieces to match the outside box lines on the squirrel, as
shown on the grid on page 19.
Cut floor 4¾x20 inches. Angle
cut the floor piece, *lengthwise,* to
fit the box sides.
    For the rabbit, cut two side
pieces measuring 6½x20 inches.
Cut two end pieces to match the
outside box lines on the rabbit, as
shown on the grid on page 18.
Cut the floor 3½x20 inches. Angle cut the floor piece, *lengthwise,*
to fit the box sides.
    Assemble the boxes with finishing nails and waterproof glue.
Bore six ¼-inch-diameter drainage holes in the floors.
    Join the ¾x10-inch redwood
pieces with a dowel or spline, to
form two workpieces that are
15x20 inches. Enlarge and transfer the pattern for the rabbit on
page 18, or the squirrel on page

19, to the ¾-inch redwood and
cut out two of the same figures
with a saber saw. Sand all edges
smooth.
    Woodburn the body details of
the animals. See page 67 for
woodburning tips.
    Attach the animal to the appropriate box ends from inside the
box, using 1¼-inch No. 6 countersunk wood screws. Position
the bottom of the box ¾ inch
above the bottom of the figure.

Herb Table Planter

Shown on page 9.

The finished table is 18½ inches
wide, 48 inches long, and 22¼
inches high.

MATERIALS
14 feet of 2x4-inch pine for legs,
    table supports, and brace
8 feet of 2x10-inch pine for
    tabletop
Four pine 1x3s, *each* 12 inches
    for cleats
Eight ¼x2½-inch zinc-treated
    screws and washers
Six ¼x3-inch zinc-treated lag
    bolts and washers
Twenty-four 1½-inch No. 8 zinc-
    treated wood screws to fasten
    the cleats
Wood putty
Oil-base wood primer
Outdoor white latex paint

INSTRUCTIONS
    CUTTING THE PARTS: Cut the
2x10s into two 4-foot pieces. The
feet and table supports are 2x4s
cut to 16½ inches. Trim a 45-degree bevel off corners of these
pieces as shown in the drawing.
Cut pads for the feet from 2x4
stock. Cut legs and horizontal
brace from 2x4 stock.
    Temporarily tack the 2x10s together with some wood strips and
finishing nails. Check alignment
of the ends with a framing square
to be sure the tabletop is square.
Lay out the hole positions by first
marking their centers. The holes

on each end have centers 6 inches from the table ends. The other hole centers are 9 inches apart.

Use a compass to draw a pattern for the 6-inch-diameter circles on a piece of paper. Push a finishing nail through the center of the pattern. Then, push the finishing nail into the crack between the two boards on one of the center line holes. Place the pattern down over the nail and scribe your line on the 2x10s. Repeat this procedure for each of the holes. Then take the boards apart and cut out the half-circles with a saber saw. Trim up the edges with a rasp; sand smooth.

ASSEMBLY: Place the 2x10s together with temporary strips and finishing nails. Then attach the 2x4 supports by countersinking the 1½-inch No. 8 wood screws in the table top.

Make 45 degree angle cuts on *each* end of the four cleats. Fasten these to the underside of the table (between the circle cutouts) with the 1½-inch No. 8 screws as shown on drawing, *below*.

Attach pads to feet with finishing nails and glue. Bolt the legs to the feet with ¼x3-inch lag bolts. Countersink the bolt heads and washers in the legs. Use washers and nuts on the inside of the feet.

Install the brace between the legs with countersunk ¼x3-inch lag bolts with the table upside down.

FINISHING: Set all nails and fill holes with wood putty. Sand the putty smooth when dry; round all table edges slightly with a medium-grade sandpaper on a sanding block. Withdraw bolts slightly and remove nuts and washers. Prime; then paint table with latex enamel. When paint is dry, reset bolts, nuts, and washers.

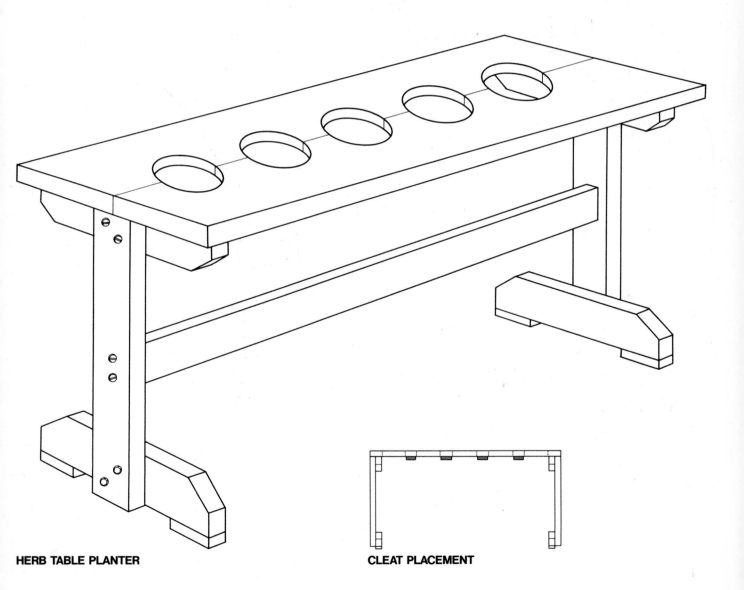

HERB TABLE PLANTER

CLEAT PLACEMENT

YARD AND DECK TRIMS

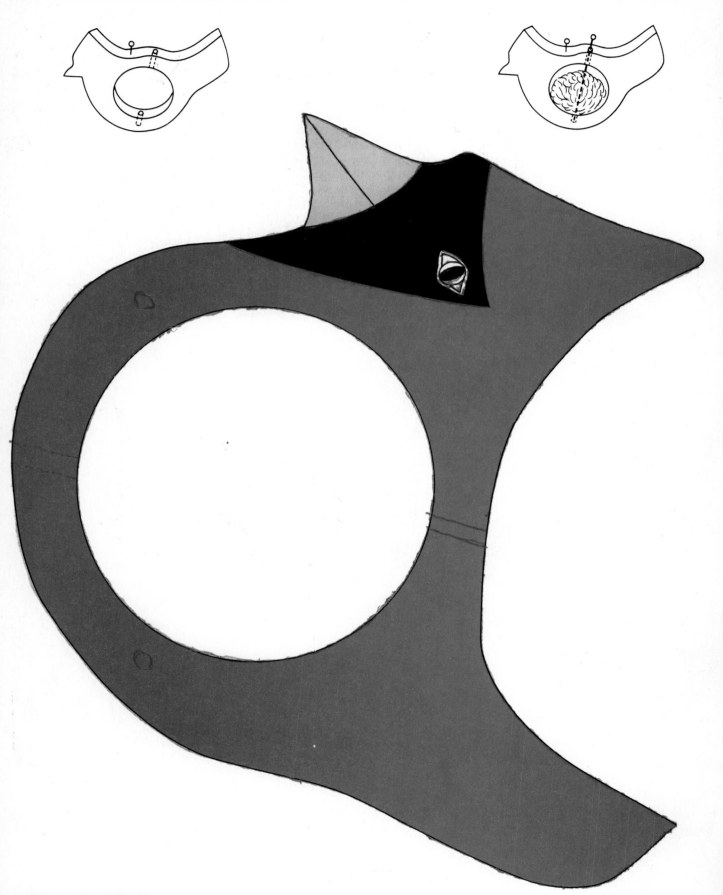

CARDINAL SUET FEEDER

GOLDFINCH SUET FEEDER

YARD AND DECK TRIMS

80°

80°

RABBIT PLANTER

1 Square = 1 Inch

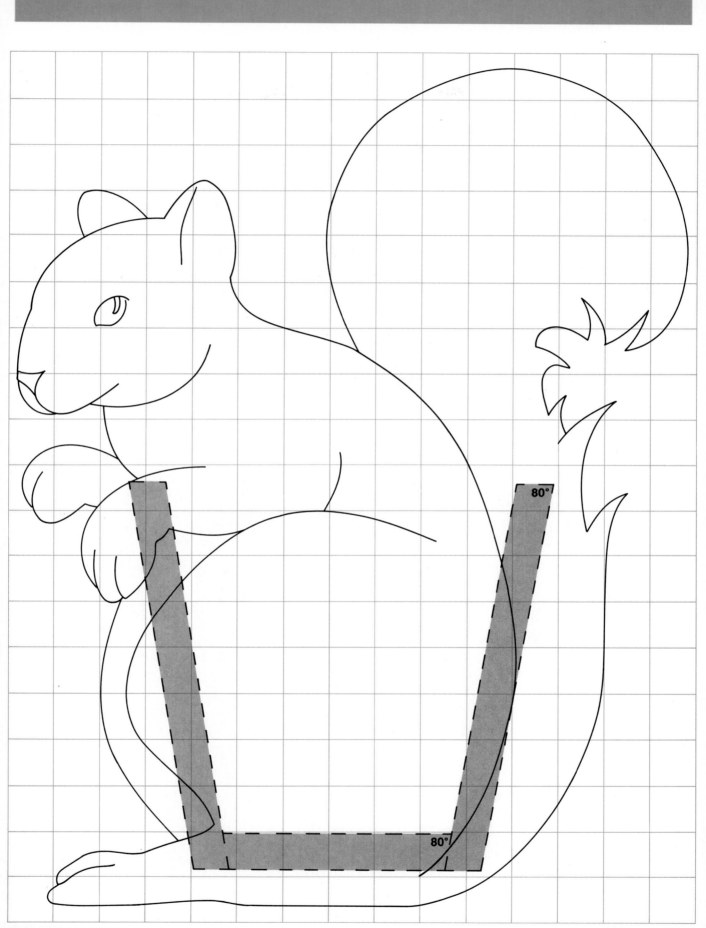

SQUIRREL PLANTER

1 Square = 1 Inch

COUNTRY ACCENTS

FOR HEARTH AND HOME

Country decorating is a style that reflects a love of home and family. With simple materials and willing hands, you can spruce up your home sweet home with all the country-style accessories in this chapter.

To set off your hearth when not in use, build the firescreen, *opposite.* Purchased wooden shutters for the side panels make its assembly a snap. Paint the hardboard inset using our design, or embellish it with a decorating motif from your room. Then frame the painted inset and add the curved trim pieces along the tops.

The amusing doorstop, *below,* will raise even the eyebrows of the cat who lives in your house. We've included detailed step-by-step painting directions for this easy project.

Instructions for the projects in this chapter begin on page 28.

COUNTRY ACCENTS

Graceful swans decorate the easy-to-build 24-inch-tall chandelier, *opposite*.

Simply cut out the swans and the rods using the full-size patterns on pages 32 and 33. Purchase the candle cups and the center pole (balluster) from a lumber supply store. After painting the pieces, coat the entire chandelier with antique glazing to bring the warmth of the old world into your home.

Complete with chimney, front and back door embellishments, and wispy curtains in the windows, the 7½-inch-tall bookends, *below* and *right,* are simple to build from scraps of lumber. You can even add your own house trims for a personal touch.

You'll love the country quaintness that the two projects on these pages will add to a tabletop or wall.

The three-dimensional tulips with their leafy foliage, *above*, add color and cheer to a kitchen, bath, or family room. Lightly sand the edges of the tulip petals and leaves after they're painted to set off their primitive charm.

To hold the tulips and leaves in place, cut and glue plastic foam to the base of your clay pot, then fill the rest of the pot with Spanish moss.

As a wonderful housewarming gift, or a bazaar best-seller, these charming tulips are always in season.

COUNTRY ACCENTS

The Shaker peg rack, *above,* is perfect for displaying all your treasured keepsakes. Made from poplar, which is stronger than pine, the 26-inch-long hanger is a single motif repeated five times. Make yours as long as you want. Then paint it in colors of your choice. Apply antique glazing for added warmth.

COUNTRY ACCENTS

The 10¾-inch-tall bookends, *opposite,* are sure to please the book-lover in your life.

Nestled in a bed of cattails, each rabbit sports a perky bow around his neck. If you love the outdoors, you'll love having this sweet woodland scene on your bookshelf. Three different thicknesses of dowels make assembling the cattails simple. The remaining portions are cut from pine and glued to a pine base. For added heft to hold heavy books, you might want to cut the rabbits and bases from scraps of oak.

After you've mastered the cattail assembly, make extras of these and the prairie grasses for fall table arrangements.

The 9½-inch table-top or shelf decoration, *above,* will find itself quite at home among all your country doodads.

All dressed up with a blue calico shawl, this proud and stately goose stands on a heart base in her wooden garden of leafy tulips.

Made from fir or pine, these shapes are easy to cut and assemble. You'll want to make lots of these to present to your country friends and neighbors.

Painted Firescreen

Shown on pages 20–21.

Firescreen measures 34½ inches high and 52 inches long.

MATERIALS
Two 12x32-inch fixed-louver-style shutters (available through Sears catalog sales)
25½x27½-inch piece of ¼-inch hardboard for the painted inset
Two 28-inch pieces of 1x3-inch pine for top and bottom framing strips of center panel
Two 26⅝-inch pieces of 1x2-inch pine for side framing strips of center panel
28 inches of 1x4-inch pine for center panel trim
Two 1-foot pieces of 1x3-inch pine for shutter panel trim
Finishing nails or ½-inch brads
1 foot of ¼-inch-diameter dowel
White primer
Acrylic paints in the following colors: dark blue, light gray, dark gray, golden yellow, brick red, green, golden brown, white, and black
Clear water-base varnish
Antique glazing

MOON MOTIF

INSTRUCTIONS
Enlarge and transfer the patterns for the contour top trim pieces on page 29 onto tracing paper; transfer patterns onto wood. Cut from wood with a saber saw.

Trim shutters to measure 31⅝ inches tall (the top and bottom frame parts of the shutters will be equal).

Join the top and bottom center frame parts to the side frame parts with dowels; then glue as shown in diagram, *bottom, right,* on page 29. Then dowel and glue the top trim pieces to the center frame and the shutter tops. Cut a ¼x½-inch rabbet in the center frame. Sand and prime all pieces.

With dark blue, paint the shutters, the framing for the screen, and the screen inset.

Enlarge and transfer the drawing, *opposite,* for the screen inset onto tracing paper. With carbon paper, transfer the drawing to the screen inset.

Referring to the photograph on pages 20 and 21, paint the areas in the background first and proceed to items in foreground. Allow paint to dry before beginning to work with the next color. Paint the curtains last with white paint, using a dry brush to achieve the airy effect and allowing the window details to show through. The small pattern on the curtain is dotted on with tip of brush. *Note:* Due to free stroking motion in painting the curtains, some repair of the bordering areas will be necessary; simply paint out the unwanted curtain detail.

Trace the full-size moon pattern, *bottom, left,* onto tracing paper; transfer pattern to the center top edge of the center framing strip. Paint the moon and your own snowflake motifs, using the photo on page 20 as a guide. Coat the painted piece with the clear varnish. Then apply the antique glazing with a soft cloth.

Attach shutters to the center frame with butt hinges. Tack the center panel in place with finishing nails or brads on back side. *Caution: Don't leave the screen in place when using the fireplace.*

Cat Doorstop

Shown on page 21.

Doorstop stands 10⅛ inches high and is 14½ inches long.

MATERIALS
15-inch length of 1x12-inch fir or pine
Scrap of 2x4-inch oak for stand
Black, yellow, green, white, flesh, and red acrylic paints
Carpenter's glue
Clear varnish
Antique glazing

INSTRUCTIONS
Enlarge and transfer cat pattern and stand on page 30 onto graph paper. Cut out patterns and transfer to wood; cut out shapes from wood.

Note: Allow each color of paint to dry before continuing with the next color.

Paint the front and side edges of the cat black. Using white carbon paper, transfer the cat body details to the front side.

For the eyes, paint the whole eye area yellow. Atop this, paint the eyes green with a black pupil. Mix green with yellow to obtain a straw color and lighten the eye around the pupil. In the upper part of the right side of the eyes, make a white dot for highlight.

Use flesh color shaded with red to paint the inner ears and nose.

For the stripes on the cat body, use a dry brush with spreading bristles. Beginning at the back end of the cat, stroke on, in striping sequence, a black and white mixture (gray) and white. Highlight the stripes with straw color. Continue across the body; refer to the photo on page 21 for a guide.

Paint around nose and mouth area, the paws, tip of the tail, and breast with white paint.

Glue stand to base of cat 2 inches from left bottom edge. Apply antique glazing to entire doorstop (to include back side). Varnish to complete.

FIRESCREEN INSET

1 Square = 2 Inches

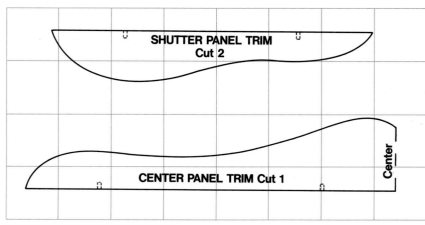

SHUTTER PANEL TRIM
Cut 2

CENTER PANEL TRIM Cut 1

Center

FIRESCREEN TOP TRIM PIECES

1 Square = 2 Inches

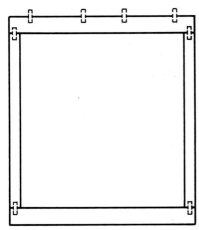

FRAME DIAGRAM

House Bookends

Shown on page 23.

Bookends stand 7½ inches high.

MATERIALS
Four 2x6-inch scraps of fir or pine, each 7½ inches long
Scraps of 1x2-inch fir or pine for chimney
Red, blue, yellow, black, green, and white acrylic paints
Carpenter's glue
Antique glazing

INSTRUCTIONS
Clamp and glue two 2x6s; repeat for the remaining two 2x6s. When dry, trim piece to 4¾ inches wide. Trace the full-size pattern of the chimney piece on page 31 onto tracing paper. Transfer the pattern to wood and cut out two chimneys.

Measure 2 inches from the tops of the glued pieces and make 120-degree angle cuts to establish the house roofs. Sand all pieces.

Using carbon paper, transfer the house back drawing, *right*, to one of the house pieces (right side of bookends). Using this drawing as a guide, draw the front side of the house on the other house piece (see the drawing, *at top,* on page 31.)

Referring to the photo on page 23, paint the roofs black, three sides of the chimneys and doors red, the upstair window areas black, and the downstairs window areas yellow. Paint the house fronts, sides, and backs blue. With a dry brush, paint white crisscross curtains in the windows; paint the door embellishments. Outline house, window, and door framings with white.

Glue one chimney to left side of the house front and the other to right side of the house back (be sure the chimneys line up with each other when they are placed together). Paint the shrubbery green around the bases of the houses and the chimneys. Apply antique glazing to all surfaces.

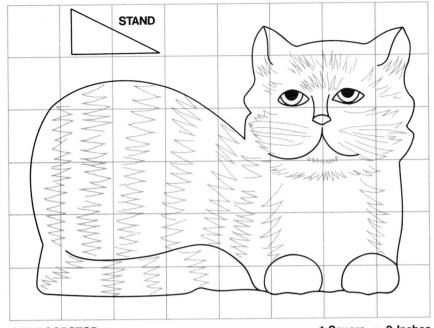

CAT DOORSTOP

1 Square = 2 Inches

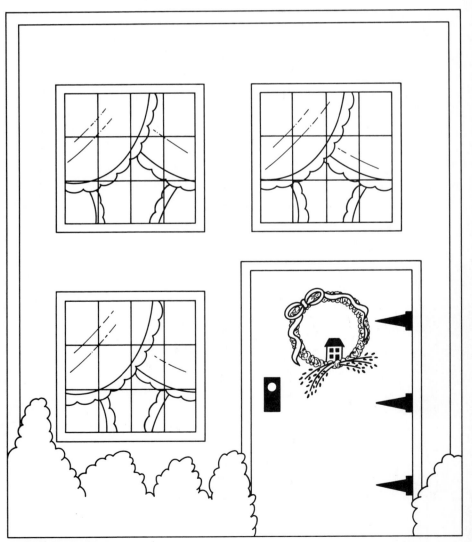

HOUSE BACK DOOR

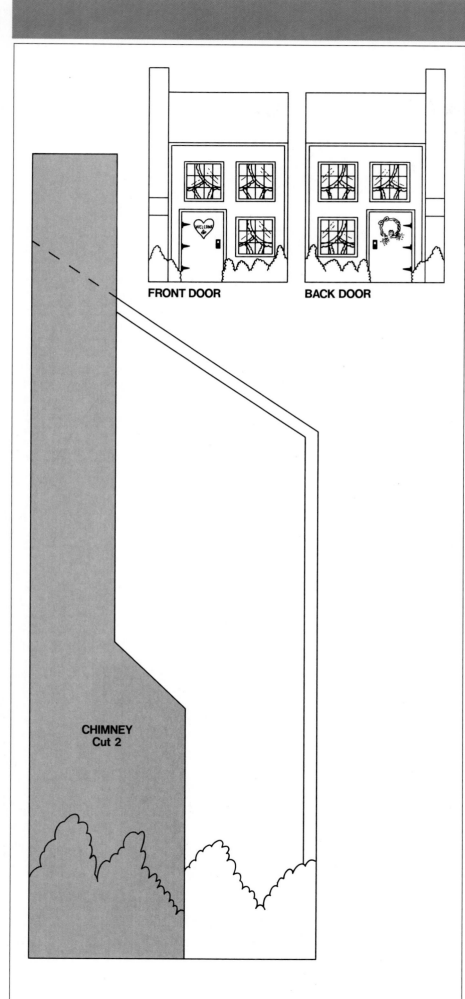

FRONT DOOR   BACK DOOR

CHIMNEY
Cut 2

Swan Chandelier

Shown on page 22.

Chandelier stands 24 inches tall.

MATERIALS
29-inch baluster (available at lumber supply stores)
Four poplar 1x10s, *each* 10½ inches long, for swans
Four poplar 1x5s, *each* 15 inches long, for rod pieces
Four candle cups
Four 1-inch No. 6 screws
Four ¼-inch-diameter dowels, *each* 1½ inches long
Eight ¼-inch-diameter dowels, *each* 1 inch long
Carpenter's glue
Wood primer
Barn red latex paint
Soft white latex paint
Antique glazing
One screw eye and chain

INSTRUCTIONS
Trace the full-size swan pattern on page 33 onto tracing paper. Align the A–B markings on the body with the A–B markings on the head to make one pattern. Transfer pattern to wood and cut out four swans.

Trace full-size rod pattern, on page 32, to include the full 11-inch length. Transfer pattern to poplar and cut out four rods.

Cut off approximately 5 inches on one end of the baluster for the top end of the chandelier; leave some of the turnings.

Center swans atop the rods and mark the dowel placements on the rods. Drill these dowel holes ⅝ inch deep. Then drill 1-inch-deep holes on ends of the rod pieces and straight edges of the baluster. Stagger the holes to prevent them from hitting each other when assembling (see diagrams, *top left*, on page 33). Drill one hole in top of each swan to attach the candle cups with screws.

Use 1½-inch dowels and glue to attach the rods to the four flat sides of the baluster.

continued

COUNTRY ACCENTS

Sand and prime all the parts. Paint the swans white; paint the candle cups and chandelier red.

Screw one candle cup atop *each* swan. Using 1-inch dowels, glue swans to the rods. Apply antique glazing to all surfaces.

Attach screw eye to top of chandelier; add desired length of chain to hang from ceiling.

Tulips in Clay Pot

Shown on page 24.

MATERIALS
Scraps of 1-inch fir or pine
6-inch-diameter clay pot
¼-inch-diameter dowels cut into 6¼-, 8-, 9¾-inch lengths
Acrylic paints in colors of your choice
Carpenter's glue
Clear spray varnish
6x6-inch piece of 2-inch-thick plastic foam
Spanish moss

INSTRUCTIONS
Trace full-size tulip and leaf patterns on page 34 onto tracing paper; transfer the patterns onto wood. *Note:* Cutting directions for tulips are for one tulip only. Cut three tulip centers and six petals to make three complete tulips.

Cut out all shapes from wood. Sand all edges smooth. Glue one petal to *each* side of one tulip center. Drill ¼-inch-diameter holes, ½ inch deep, in bottoms of tulip centers. Paint tulips desired colors. Paint leaves and dowels green. Glue tulips to tops of dowels. For a rustic look, sand just the edges of the leaves and tulips; then spray all the surfaces with the clear varnish.

Cut plastic foam to fit bottom of clay pot and glue it in place. Position tulips and leaves in place. Fill pot with Spanish moss.

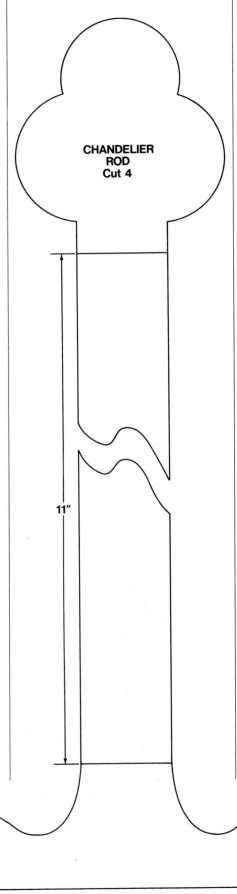

CHANDELIER ROD
Cut 4

11"

Tulip Wall Hanger

Shown on page 25.

Hanger is 6 inches high and 26 inches long.

MATERIALS
28 inches of 1x8-inch poplar
Five 2½-inch Shaker pegs
Wood primer
Red, green, pink, and black acrylic paints or colors of your choice
Antique glazing
Carpenter's glue
Two picture hangers

INSTRUCTIONS
Trace the full-size tulip pattern on page 35 onto tracing paper. Draw a straight line along length of wood 1 inch from its bottom edge. Trace 5 tulip motifs in a row onto the wood piece, having edges of leaves touching and bottom curve resting on straight line (see diagram, *at bottom,* on page 35).

Cut out the tulip piece from wood. Using ⅜-inch drill bit, drill ⅝-inch-deep holes in center of leaves of each tulip for the Shaker pegs. Sand and prime the tulip piece and the Shaker pegs.

Referring to the photo on page 25, paint the tulip piece and the pegs. To define the stem shape, paint the small triangular shapes on either sides of the stems with black. Darken the tulip and leaf colors with black and outline the leaves and tulips if desired. Apply the antique glazing according to the manufacturer's directions.

Glue pegs into drilled holes; then center and add hangers to first and last tulip motifs on the back side.

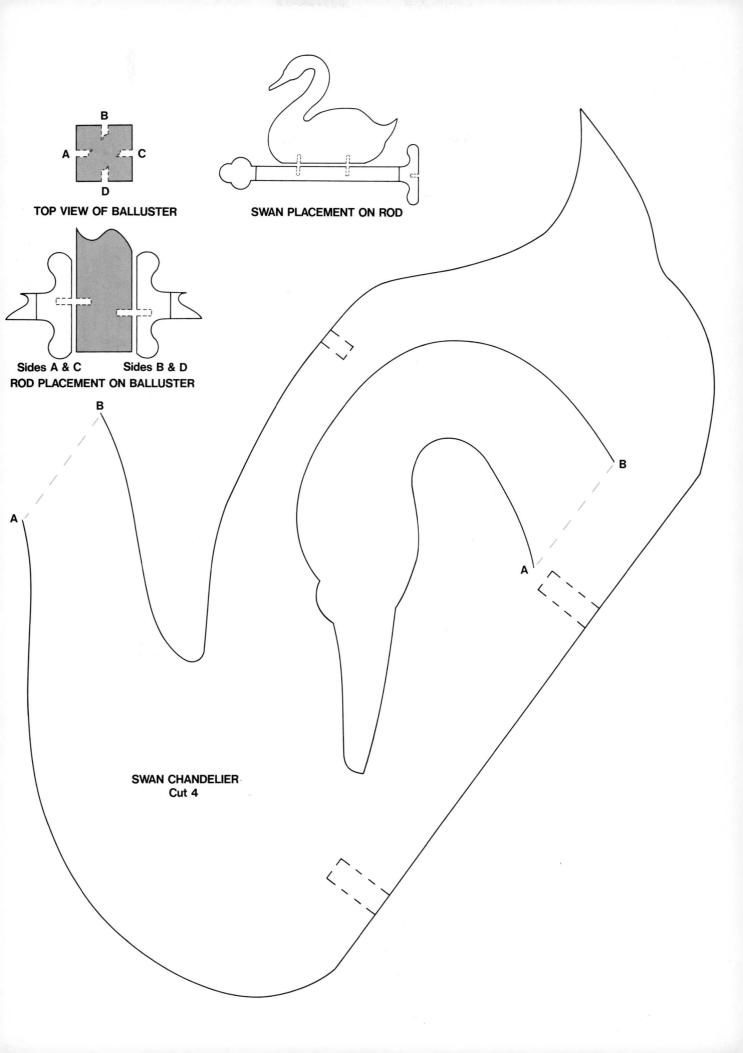

TOP VIEW OF BALLUSTER

B
A   C
D

SWAN PLACEMENT ON ROD

Sides A & C   Sides B & D

ROD PLACEMENT ON BALLUSTER

B

A

B

A

SWAN CHANDELIER
Cut 4

Rabbit Bookends

Shown on page 27.

Bookends stand 10¾ inches tall and are 8 inches long.

MATERIALS
For the set
One 16-inch length of 2x8-inch fir or pine for rabbits
One 16-inch length 1x4-inch fir or pine for bases
Scraps of 1-inch fir or pine
Two 7-inch lengths of ¼-inch-diameter dowels for cattail stems
Two 1½-inch lengths of $\frac{1}{16}$-inch-diameter dowels for cattail tips
Two 3-inch lengths of ¾-inch-diameter dowels for cattails
Wood stain in desired color
Green acrylic paint
Clear spray varnish
Carpenter's glue or hot-glue gun
Two 20-inch lengths of plaid taffeta ribbon

INSTRUCTIONS
Trace the full-size grass and rabbit patterns on page 36 onto tracing paper; then transfer the rabbit pattern onto 2x8-inch fir; cut two. Cut the 1x4-inch fir into two pieces to make two 8-inch-long bases. Cut two of *each* grass blade from scraps of 1-inch fir. Sand all rough edges.

Paint the bases, ¼-inch dowels, and grass blades green. For a rustic look, sand just the edges after the paint is dry.

To make cattails, drill $\frac{1}{16}$-inch hole in one end and ¼-inch hole in opposite end of the ¾-inch dowels. Sand the top and bottom edges of the dowels to round the corners and sand the sides to give added texture.

Glue $\frac{1}{16}$-inch dowel in one end of the cattail dowel and sand the exposed end of this dowel to a soft point.

Stain the rabbits and the cattails the desired color.

Using the photograph on page 27 as a guide, position the rabbits on the bases so the tails are even

with one of the side edges and sit back about 1 inch from the front edge of the base. Position grass blades and glue in place. Drill ¼-inch hole (one on each base) with a slight angle behind blades of grass. Glue ¼-inch dowels into cattails and bases.

Spray with clear varnish when all glue is dry. Tie ribbons around necks of rabbits.

Goose on Heart Base

Shown on page 26.

Decoration stands 9½ inches tall.

MATERIALS
Scraps of 1-inch fir or poplar or ½-inch pine scraps, if available
9-inch length of ¼-inch-diameter dowel rod
White, green, blue, red, yellow, and black acrylic paints
Wood stain in desired color for heart base
6x6-inch square of calico fabric
Clear spray varnish
Glue gun or carpenter's glue

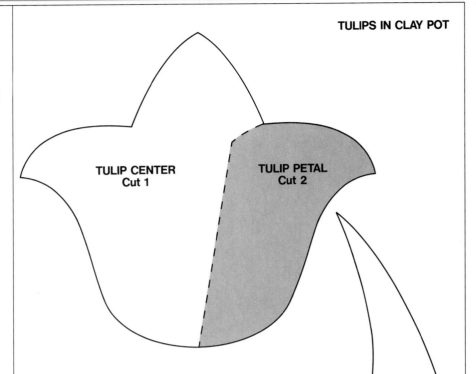

TULIPS IN CLAY POT

TULIP CENTER
Cut 1

TULIP PETAL
Cut 2

LEAF
Cut 3

INSTRUCTIONS

Trace full-size patterns on page 37 onto tracing paper; then transfer patterns onto wood. Cut out all shapes. Sand all edges smooth. Referring to the phototgraph on page 26, stain the heart and paint the remaining shapes (goose, tulips, and leaves).

From dowel, cut the following lengths: one 2¾-inch length for goose, one 2½-inch length for the blue tulip, one 2-inch length for the red tulip, and one 1½-inch length for the yellow tulip. Paint dowel for goose white; paint dowels for tulips green.

Drill ¼-inch-deep holes in bottoms of tulips and goose. Glue dowels to their matching pieces.

Using heart pattern as a placement guide, drill ¼-inch-deep holes in heart base for placement of goose and tulips; glue all pieces in place, including leaves. Spray entire piece with clear varnish after glue is set and dry.

Fold fabric in half to make a triangular shawl and tie around the neck of the goose.

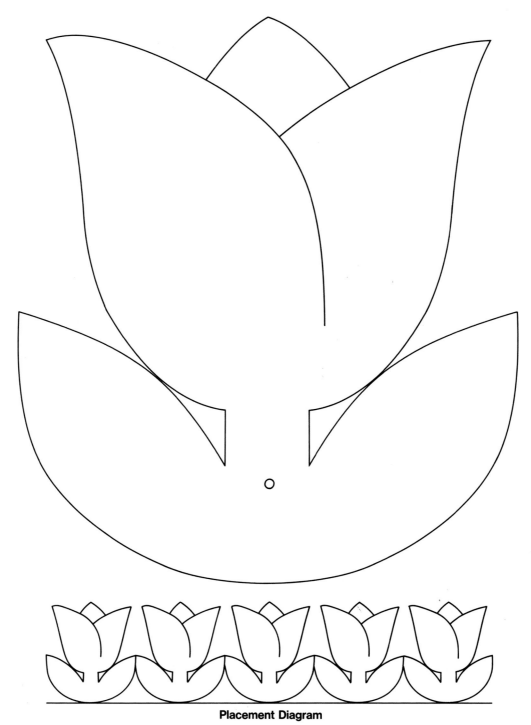

Placement Diagram

TULIP WALL HANGER

COUNTRY ACCENTS

Sandpaper Grades and Their Uses

Sandpaper may be the most familiar finishing tool for woodworking. And the interesting thing about sandpaper is that the sand isn't really sand, and the paper isn't really paper, but a composition material. When properly selected, sandpaper can save you plenty of time and effort on many of your crafts projects.

Sandpaper (technically, a coated abrasive) is available in grades ranging from 24 for coarse sanding to 600 for very fine sanding. Most woodcrafting requires sandpaper in the range from 80 to 280. For medium, or first sanding, use grades 80, 100, or 120. Use grades 150, 180, or 220 for fine or second sanding. And for very fine sanding, or third sanding, use grades 220, 240, or 280.

Sandpaper selection is easy. Most manufacturers label the package for the sandpaper's intended use, such as "For Metal," "For Hardwoods." Manufacturers also indicate the coarseness of the sheets and the number of sheets the package contains. For example, you might see a package labeled, "2 fine, 2 medium, 1 coarse."

Do not cut sandpapers with a knife or scissors. Cutting sandpaper dulls the edges of these tools. Instead, score the paper or cloth side with an awl or nail. Then crease it by folding the paper over and tear it along the creased line.

Store these papers in a cool, dry place, laying them flat so the sheets do not curl. Use the sheets until no abrasiveness is left. Save *slightly* worn paper for later use.

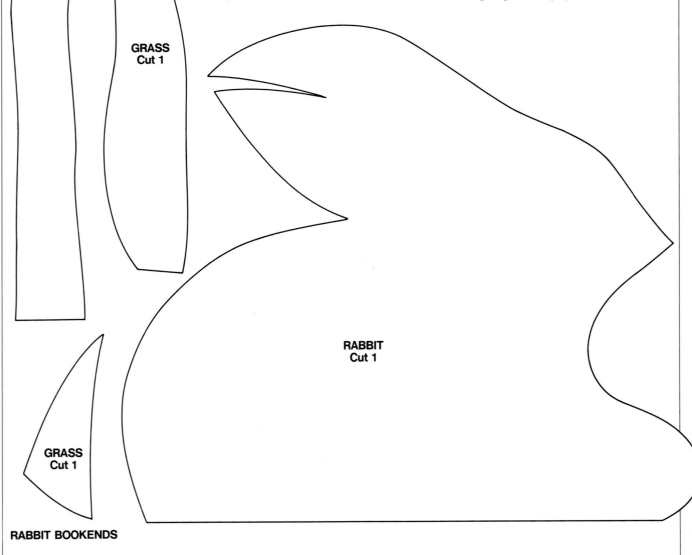

GRASS
Cut 1

GRASS
Cut 1

GRASS
Cut 1

RABBIT
Cut 1

RABBIT BOOKENDS

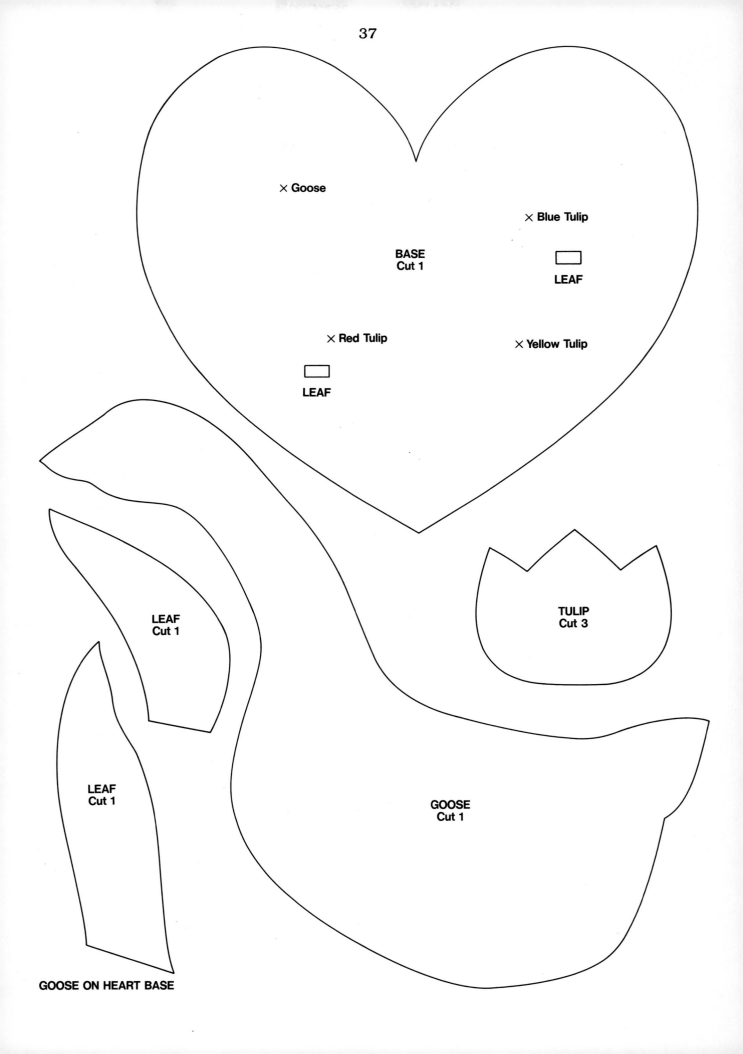

× Goose

× Blue Tulip

BASE
Cut 1

LEAF

× Red Tulip

× Yellow Tulip

LEAF

LEAF
Cut 1

TULIP
Cut 3

LEAF
Cut 1

GOOSE
Cut 1

GOOSE ON HEART BASE

TOYS AND GAMES

JUST FOR KIDS

When it comes to winning a youngster's affection, you surely won't miss when you make any one of the projects in this chapter. Crafted from sturdy materials and painted with cheerful colors, this collection of playthings is designed to take lots of wear and tear and bring endless hours of enjoyment.

This little girl tenderly rocks her tiny baby to sleep in the enchanting 26-inch-long cradle, *opposite.*

Built from ½-inch plywood, the cradle features head- and footboards that are splendid poses of the elegant swan. A rocker bar, to rock the cradle by hand or foot, is reminiscent of cradles long ago.

Make yours as we did, or use just one of the swan patterns for both the head- and footboards and reverse the directions of their heads so the cradle balances properly.

The LOVE letters, *above,* with their frolicking bear embellishments, express your feelings for a special tot.

Whether you set them on a shelf or hang them on a wall, these playful letters are also delightful beginnings for a child who's learning to recognize letters.

Full-size patterns for the letters make them easy to transfer to wood, cut out, and paint.

For another painted version of these letters, refer to pages 60-61.

How-to instructions for all the projects in this chapter begin on page 46.

TOYS AND GAMES

These 8½-inch-diameter animal puzzles will entertain youngsters for hours.

Whether your children choose to make the lion, dog, or pig as shown in the photo, *above,* or create their own monster animals, *left,* these mix-and-match shapes will provide lots of creative play for bright little minds.

Made from scraps of wood, these three puzzles are crafted from simple cut shapes, embellished with acrylic paints, and sprayed with a coat of varnish.

Each puzzle has an identically shaped piece for its mouth, facial features, tail, and body. Simply by interchanging the pieces of each puzzle, kids can create funny new animals.

Use the pattern pieces and create even goofier puzzles. Add your own drawings—caricature faces of your family members, clown faces, or ball designs, such as baseball, basketball, and soccer—atop the pieces and paint with bright and lively colors.

TOYS AND GAMES

Young and old alike will love the rocking motion of the pull toy, *above*. Constructed from scraps of walnut and oak and colorful purchased wooden beads, this walking toy is the funniest sight on wheels.

Sturdy string is threaded through the tail, body parts, and head for easy assembly. Allow enough string for pulling, then knot the string and pull it through the handle bead.

The cat and mouse ticktacktoe set, *opposite,* will bring lots of excitement to this old and favorite game.

Construct the 20-inch-long playing board from fir or pine and cut the cat and mouse playing pieces from ¼-inch pine window casing. Then paint the board and playing pieces as shown, or in colors of your choice.

Hang the board on a wall for easy storage. String the playing pieces onto a shoelace that dangles from the cat's tail.

TOYS AND GAMES

If you're looking for a sure-to-please present for a junior woodworker, you can't go wrong with the child-size workbench, *left*. Built just like dad's, it measures 16 inches wide, 49½ inches long, and is 24 inches tall.

Painted a bright blue, or your child's favorite color, this bench has lots of work space on top and a bottom shelf for storing lumber and projects in progress.

The top of the table is finished with a hardboard piece that lies on a plywood base. When the top is worn out, it easily can be removed and replaced.

You can change the height of the bench by adjusting the lengths of the 2x3s used for the legs if your child needs a working level that is higher than 24 inches. You'll want to make this change before buying and cutting the lumber as it is listed in the materials list on page 52.

Use nylon cording (available at sporting goods stores), fastened with finishing washers and screws, to make tool holders on one end of the bench, as shown in the photo, *above*. Allow enough gap in the cording as it is fastened to the bench to hold the child-size tools.

Step-by-step instructions, with drawings that demonstrate assembly, make this project one that can be built in an evening or two in your workshop.

TOYS AND GAMES

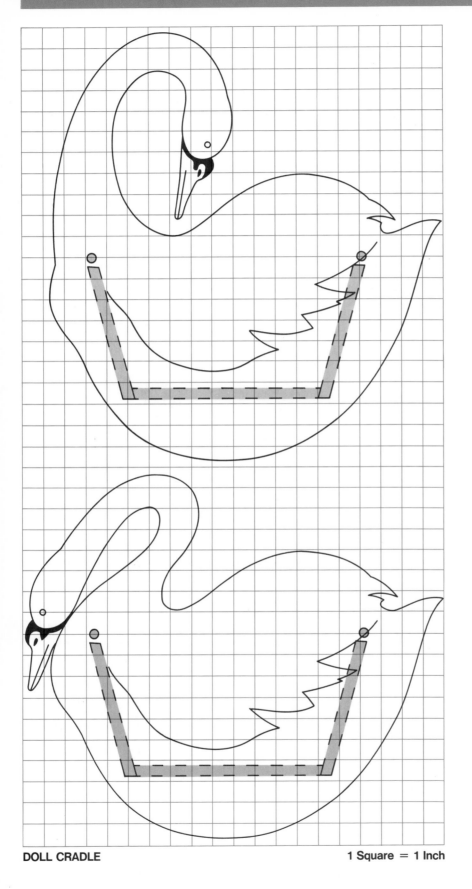

DOLL CRADLE   1 Square = 1 Inch

Swan Doll Cradle

Shown on page 38.

Cradle stands 20 inches tall; it is 18½ inches wide and 26 inches long.

MATERIALS
4x4-foot piece of ½-inch plywood
Two ½-inch-diameter dowels, each 25½ inches long
Carpenter's glue
Four plastic eyes (available in crafts supply stores)
White primer paint
White, black, and orange enamel paints
Finishing nails; wood filler

INSTRUCTIONS
Enlarge patterns for the cradle head- and footboards, *left.* Transfer patterns to plywood and cut out. Fill edges and sand lightly.

Note: One pattern can be used for both head- and footboard, if desired.

Cut two 6½x25-inch pieces for cradle sides; angle bottom edges 15 degrees. Cut a 9x25-inch piece for cradle floor; angle sides 15 degrees. Glue and nail sides to floor.

Drill ½-inch-diameter holes in head- and footboards ¼ inch deep for dowels (see diagram for placement). Position swan head- and footboards to assembled base, referring to pattern for placement; glue dowels into place. Fasten cradle to footboards with countersunk nails and glue. Secure dowel rails in place with nails from the outside of the head- footboards.

Cover nail holes with wood filler; sand smooth. Prime all surfaces. Paint cradle, adding details. Drill holes and set eyes in place on each side of swans.

LOVE Letters

Shown on page 39.

Tallest letter is 10¾ inches; all others are 7¾ inches.

MATERIALS

3½ feet of 1x8-inch pine
Watercolor paintbrushes
Acrylic paints in the following colors: white, blue, yellow, green, pink, lavender, brown, black, and white

INSTRUCTIONS

Refer to page 70 for the instructions for cutting out the letter shapes and pages 73–75 for the letter patterns for the L, O, and E. The pattern for letter V is *below*.

Use the photograph on page 39 as a guide for painting the details.

LOVE LETTERS

TOYS AND GAMES

Animal Puzzles

Shown on pages 40–41.

All the puzzles are 8½ inches in diameter.

MATERIALS
Scraps of 1-inch pine or fir
White primer
Acrylic paints in the following colors: yellow, orange, pink, white, black, red, dark blue, and light blue
Spray varnish

INSTRUCTIONS
Trace full-size pattern pieces, *right,* and on page 49, onto tracing paper and transfer the patterns onto the wood scraps. Cut three of *each* pattern piece to make the three animal puzzles. Sand smooth all edges and prime all surfaces.

Enlarge the drawings for the three animals, *below,* onto graph paper. Using graphite paper, transfer design lines onto the appropriate wood pieces. *Note:* The gray lines on the drawings indicate the separations for the puzzle pieces.

Paint the animals, using the photographs as a guide. Lighten or darken colors with white or black to obtain shades of blue and pink. For ease in painting, allow each color to dry before painting adjacent colors. Paint side edges and the back sides with the main color of the corresponding animal. When completely dry, spray all pieces with varnish.

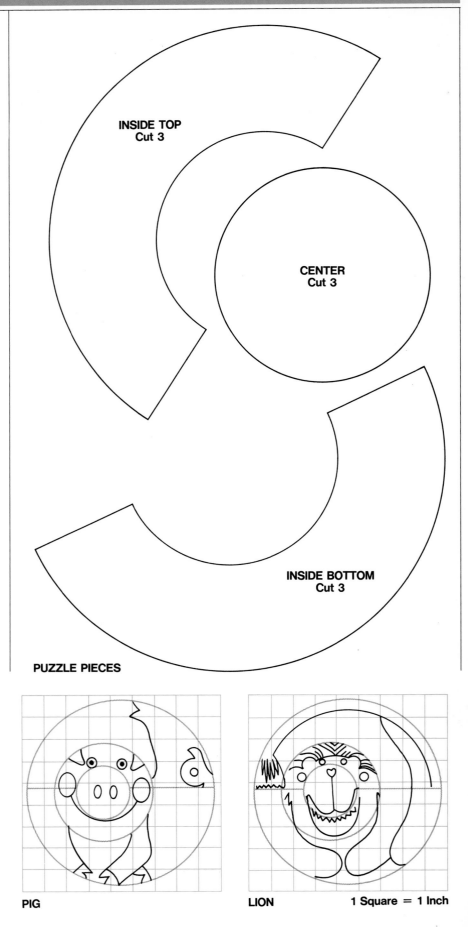

INSIDE TOP
Cut 3

CENTER
Cut 3

INSIDE BOTTOM
Cut 3

PUZZLE PIECES

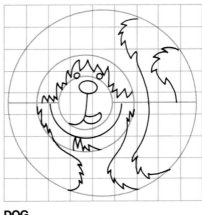

DOG

PIG

LION

1 Square = 1 Inch

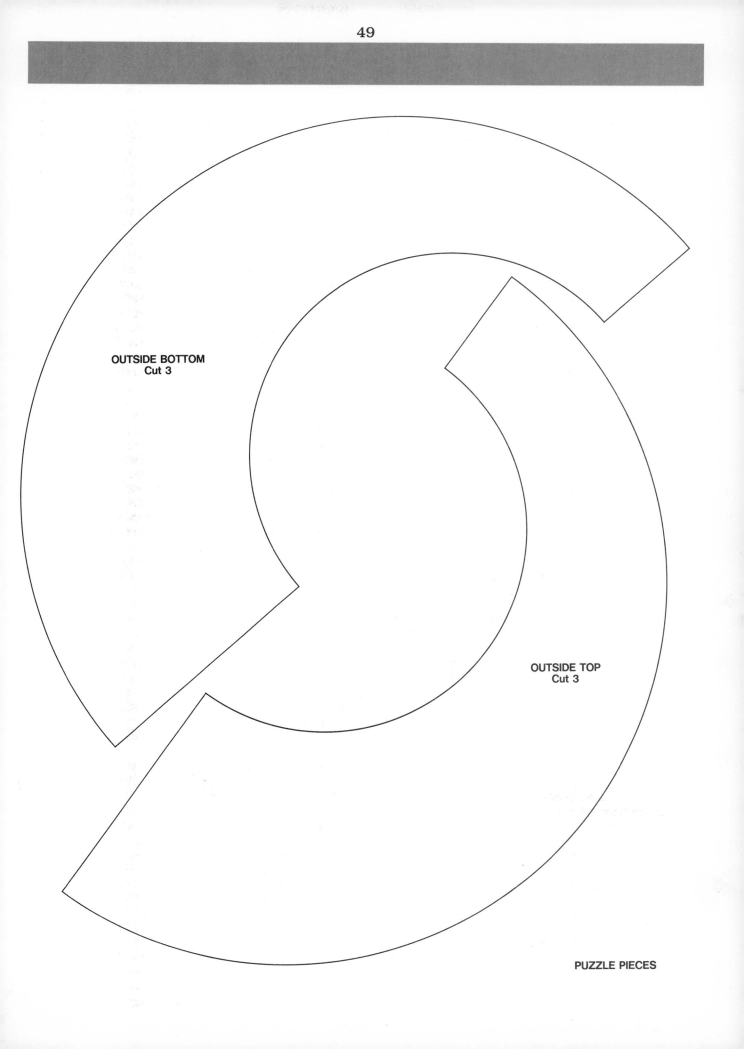

OUTSIDE BOTTOM
Cut 3

OUTSIDE TOP
Cut 3

PUZZLE PIECES

Cat and Mouse Ticktacktoe

Shown on page 43.

The cat playing board is 20 inches tall.

MATERIALS
12x21-inch piece of 1-inch fir or
  pine
12 inches of ¼-inch pine
  window casing
Black, white, and yellow acrylic
  paints
Clear spray varnish
Crafts glue
Gray buttonhole twist
Thin black 27-inch shoelace
Picture hanger

INSTRUCTIONS
Enlarge the cat board, *right,* onto folded graph paper. Add the tail on the right side of the cat by aligning the A-B dashed line on the cat with the A-B line on the tail. Do not extend the tail on the left side. Transfer the markings to the 1-inch fir; cut shape from wood. Sand smooth all edges.

Trace five mice and five cat full-size playing pieces onto the ¼-inch pine window casing; cut out. Sand smooth all edges.

Using a ⅛-inch drill bit, drill a hole in each cat and mouse (black dot on pattern). With a 1/16-inch drill bit, drill a hole in the back end of each mouse to hold the tail.

Using the photograph on page 42 as a guide, paint board and playing pieces. When paint is dry, add the facial details to all pieces. Spray all pieces with varnish.

Cut five 4-inch pieces of buttonhole twist and glue into small hole in each mouse for tail.

For ease in storing, attach picture hanger to back of cat board for hanging.

String the cats and mice onto the shoelace and tie the ends together. Hang lace from the tail to store until ready to play.

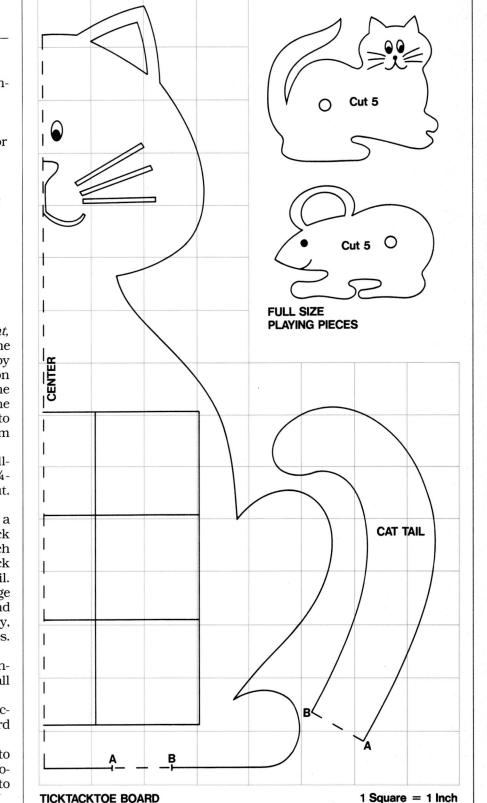

Cut 5

Cut 5

FULL SIZE PLAYING PIECES

CENTER

CAT TAIL

B

A

A   B

TICKTACKTOE BOARD

1 Square = 1 Inch

Wooden Beaded Pull Toy

Shown on page 42.

Toy is approximately 11 inches long from head to tail.

MATERIALS
Scraps of ¾-inch oak for head and wheels
Scraps of ¾-inch walnut for body
Miscellaneous wooden beads for connectors, tail, and pull
Two 2½-inch long dowels, *each* ¼-inch in diameter for axles
Scrap of red felt for tongue
Carpenter's glue; clear varnish
Black and white acrylic paints
48 inches of string or cord

INSTRUCTIONS
Trace full-size pattern for head and wheels, *bottom, right,* onto tracing paper. Transfer patterns to oak and cut five pieces. Cut out the colored wedge on one of the pieces to make the head. Trace pattern for the body; transfer pattern to walnut; cut two pieces.

Drill ⅛-inch-diameter holes through head and body pieces for string using the narrow dashed lines on patterns as a guide. Drill ¼-inch-diameter holes through both body pieces for dowel axles, using the wide dashed lines as a guide. Refer to both the top and side view of the body patterns for placement of these holes.

Drill ¼-inch-diameter holes, ¼ inch deep into center of *each* wheel. Drill ⅛-inch-diameter hole in center of one side of the handle bead. Sand smooth all pieces.

Paint eyes onto head piece. Varnish all pieces. When dry, glue the felt tongue in place.

Insert a wood dowel through *each* body square. The dowels should move easily in and out the holes. Glue the wheels to ends of the dowels, making sure the left wheel on each axle is perpendicular to the right wheel so the toy "walks" when pulled.

Assemble the toy by first knotting one end of the string and pulling it through the tail beads, through one body piece, through bead connector, through second body piece, through another bead connector, through the head, and through the ⅛-inch diameter hole of the pull (handle) bead and out through the opening at one end of this bead. See the diagram, *below,* for ease in assembly. Allow enough string for pulling. Knot the end and pull it back into the bead to finish the threading.

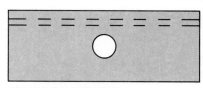

SIDE VIEW OF BODY

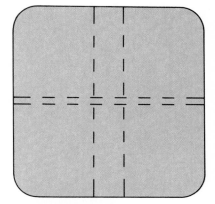

TOP VIEW OF BODY

PULL TOY ASSEMBLY

HEAD / WHEEL

Child's Workbench

Shown on pages 44–45.

Workbench measures 16 inches wide, 49½ inches long, and 24 inches high.

MATERIALS
14½x48 inches of ¼-inch tempered hardboard for top
14½x48 inches of ½-inch plywood for top shelf
14x45 inches of ½-inch plywood for bottom shelf
16½x45 inches of plywood for backboard
Four pine 2x3s, *each* 23¼-inches, for legs
Two pine 1x4s, *each* 49½ inches, and two pine 1x4s, *each* 14½-inches, for top apron
Two pine 1x3s, *each* 45-inches, and two pine 1x3s, *each* 12½-inches, for bottom apron
Two pine 1x2s, *each* 45-inches, and two pine 1x2s, *each* 9½-inches, for cleats
Thirty-six 1-inch No. 8 wood screws
Twelve 2-inch No. 8 zinc-treated wood screws
6d finishing nails
¾-inch No. 17 brads
Wood primer and stain
Clear varnish
Blue enamel paint
16 inches of 1-inch-wide blue nylon strapping
Six No. 8 finishing washers
Six ¾-inch No. 8 flat head wood screws
Child-size tools

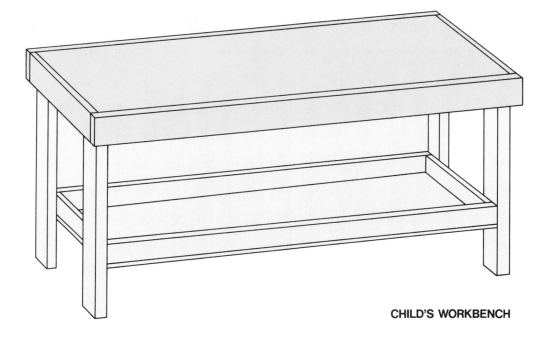

CHILD'S WORKBENCH

INSTRUCTIONS
Cut all parts of the workbench, except the hardboard top, to sizes given in the materials list. Attach 1x2 cleats to the 1x4s that form the top frame. The cleats stop short of the long piece ends by 2¼ inches and the short piece ends by 3½ inches. Use finishing nails to attach the cleats. Also use glue here and in all assembly steps, except where noted otherwise.

Then assemble the 1x4s with butt joints and 6d finishing nails.

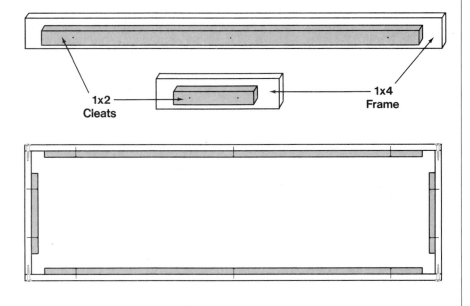

1x2 Cleats

1x4 Frame

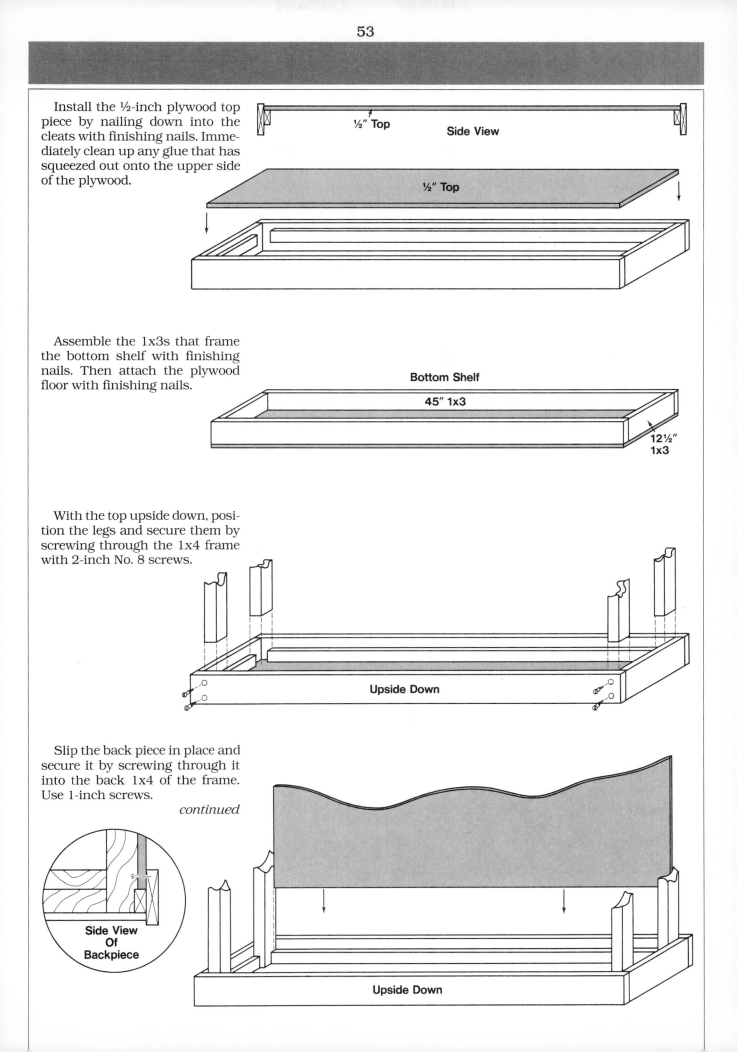

Install the ½-inch plywood top piece by nailing down into the cleats with finishing nails. Immediately clean up any glue that has squeezed out onto the upper side of the plywood.

½" Top
Side View

½" Top

Assemble the 1x3s that frame the bottom shelf with finishing nails. Then attach the plywood floor with finishing nails.

Bottom Shelf
45" 1x3
12½" 1x3

With the top upside down, position the legs and secure them by screwing through the 1x4 frame with 2-inch No. 8 screws.

Upside Down

Slip the back piece in place and secure it by screwing through it into the back 1x4 of the frame. Use 1-inch screws.

continued

Side View Of Backpiece

Upside Down

Position the bottom shelf and attach it to the legs 5 inches from the floor, with 2-inch screws from the inside of the 1x3s. Also screw through the back plywood piece into the back of the 1x3s with 1-inch screws.

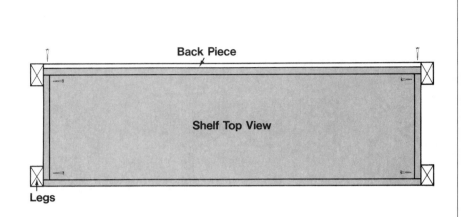

Back Piece

Shelf Top View

Legs

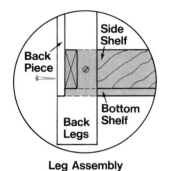

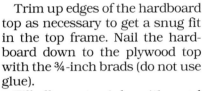

Leg Assembly

Trim up edges of the hardboard top as necessary to get a snug fit in the top frame. Nail the hardboard down to the plywood top with the ¾-inch brads (do not use glue).

Fill all countersinks with wood putty and sand smooth. Lightly round all surface edges using medium-grade sandpaper wrapped around a sanding block.

Prime all surfaces except the top and its frame. Then paint in primary colors. Stain the frame to match the color of the hardboard and then coat both with varnish.

With a lighted match, burn even one edge of the nylon strapping. Referring to photo on page 45, fasten the strapping to one short side of the workbench. Use your child's tools to determine the spacing and the amount of slack necessary to hold the tools. Secure in place with the finishing washers and the ¾-inch flat head screws. Burn the remaining end and secure it in place. *Note:* Burning melts the nylon and prevents it from fraying.

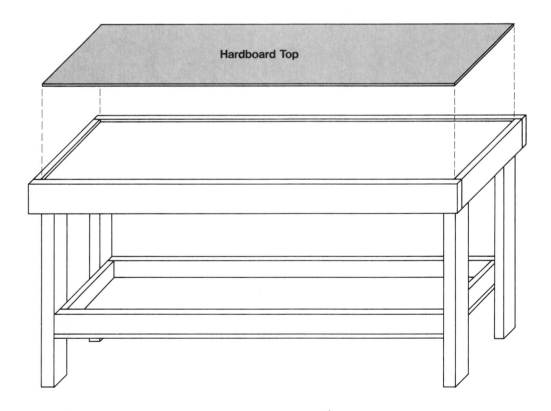

Hardboard Top

Shopping for Wood

Before you visit the lumberyard to buy materials for all your woodworking projects, you need to know a bit about wood and its properties. For example, lumber is either a *softwood*, from evergreen trees or a *hardwood*, from deciduous trees. Also, all pieces of lumber have a *nominal* set of dimensions and an *actual* set. Below you'll find information on selecting and purchasing wood. Keep in mind that most of the projects in this book are crafted from softwoods.

Softwoods

Pine has been largely replaced by fir as the leading softwood. Even when you ask for pine, many lumberyards will give you fir. Fir is far less expensive than pine, but its woodworking qualities are similar.

GRADING LUMBER: There is a system for grading wood according to its qualities, but for most of your woodworking projects you can easily pick the quality you need by eye. Avoid cracked and warped boards and boards with lots of milling stubble. Check both sides of the board and do not purchase boards with large knots, or boards with holes where the knots have fallen out.

CHOOSING THE RIGHT SIZE: Many lumberyards or home center stores price lumber by the piece. This is perfect for the person who wants just one board, with a particular dimension.

Wood pieces that are less than 2 inches thick and 3 inches wide are called *strips*. Wood pieces that are less than 2 inches thick and more than 3 inches wide are called *boards*. *Dimension lumber* is wood that is 2 inches thick and 2 or more inches wide. Studs and planks are types of dimension lumber.

When talking to a lumber supply salesperson, remember that the thickness and width of a piece of wood is actually smaller than the size by which it is sold. For example, lumber sold as a 2x4-inch piece is actually a 1½x3½-inch piece. Purchase lumber for the exact size of your needs even if you need to buy the next standard size.

Follow the chart below when ordering wood, keeping in mind that in woodworking nomenclature, nominal dimensions are larger than actual size.

STANDARD LUMBER SIZES	
Nominal Size	Actual Size in Inches
STRIPS	
1x2	¾x1½
1x3	¾x2½
BOARDS	
1x4	¾x3½
1x6	¾x5½
1x8	¾x7¼
1x10	¾x9¼
1x12	¾x11¼
DIMENSION LUMBER	
2x2	1½x1½
2x3	1½x2½
2x4	1½x3½
2x6	1½x5½
2x8	1½x7¼
2x10	1½x9¼
2x12	1½x11¼

Hardwoods

Among hardwoods, oak is most often used by woodworkers. Other beautiful and strong hardwoods include ash, mahogany, poplar, maple, walnut, and teak.

These woods are far more expensive and in shorter supply than softwoods. When shopping for hardwoods, keep in mind that they are cut into random lengths and widths when harvested, to make the best possible use of all the available wood. Hardwood usually comes 1 inch to 2 inches thick, but it's also often available in ½-inch thicknesses, making it handy for small projects.

Like softwoods, hardwood lumber also has both nominal and actual dimensions. So when you order a 1-inch piece of stock, the piece you get won't quite measure one inch thick.

Look for bargains in used lumber, too. You may find it at the wrecking site of an old building, or see it advertised in the classified section of your newspaper. Used lumber may look old and dirty, but often you'll find strong, seasoned wood free of bad defects beneath the coat of grime.

Composition materials

Of all the compostition materials, plywood, which is strong, lightweight, and easy to work, is the one used most often. It is made of thin sheets of wood glued together. It is sold in 4-foot by 8-foot sheets that range from ⅛ to ¾ inch thick. If you are painting your project, buy birch veneer plywood. It has one good side for painting. If you are staining, you may prefer the more expensive hardwood veneer plywood.

Some stores sell plywood in sections smaller than the 4x8 sheets, but you often pay almost as much for a section as for a full sheet. Compare prices before you buy less than half a sheet. Don't worry about purchasing a little more than you need; the leftover piece will come in handy sooner or later.

HARDBOARD: Hardboard also comes in 4x8 sheets in thicknesses from ⅛ to 5/16 inch in ⅛-inch increments.

Constructed from wood fibers that are pressed together under great pressure, hardboards are of two types—standard and tempered. Tempered hardboard is stronger and a darker shade of brown than the standard version. Its pressed fiber makeup yields a dense and smooth product that paints well and won't splinter or crack.

PARTICLEBOARD: This material is also made from wood particles that are pressed into sheets. Particleboard is fairly dense, extremely heavy, and smooth on both sides. It tends to chip and break easily; be sure to protect its edges with sturdy framing.

Crafters often consider particleboard unsuitable for many crafts projects. Examine some samples and make up your own mind.

A CHRISTMAS CELEBRATION

WITH SIMPLE DELIGHTS

Show off your holiday spirit with simple, but beautifully designed and crafted, Christmas trims. For starters, make this partridge-in-a-pear-tree wreath for a table, entry, or mantel. Then try the other projects featured on the next three pages.

The peaceful 16½-inch tabletop decoration, *left,* sets the mood for a glowing Christmas Eve. The partridge settled in its humble nest and surrounded by golden pears offers a memorable decoration for a buffet dinner.

Our circular tree is built on a plywood base with strips of pine lath laid in a chevron across its top. The pears, bird, and nest are simple shapes, cut from hardboard, that are easily painted with acrylics. The "rickrack" trim encircling the edges is 1⅛-inch squares of lath that are stapled to the back. Grape vine twigs, glued atop the hardboard nest, complete its assembly.

You also can use this decoration as a festive door trim. Add boughs of greenery around its edges and a large plaid bow to stream from the base of the nest.

How-to instructions for the the projects in this chapter begin on page 64.

A CHRISTMAS CELEBRATION

Many families follow the lovely tradition of making small manger scenes to display in their homes during the Christmas season.

Simple materials are appropriate for a humble nativity setting. Fir plywood is used for the artful crèche figures on these two pages. The arch stands 10½ inches tall, and all of the remaining pieces are proportionately scaled to match.

Full-size patterns for all of the figures make cutting easy. Woodburn the details (the heavy black lines), and apply wood stains to define shapes and parts of the figures as shown on the crèche, *opposite;* or apply diluted acrylics to color the figures as shown, *below.*

Children especially love to create trims for Christmas. After you cut out the pieces, you might let the kids define the outline with a brown marker pen and color the figures with felt-tip pens.

The jolly 4¼-inch-tall snowman tree ornaments, *opposite*, are all dressed for Christmas with their red plaid scarves and hat trims of holly and berries.

Craft their bodies from ¼-inch hardboard and drill tiny holes in their sides to hold the twig arms. You'll want to make lots of these fellows to give as gifts to neighbors and friends.

These festive painted letters with their busy bear embellishments can dance across your fireplace mantel as easily as they dance across our pages. They'll look equally splendid arranged in a centerpiece on your holiday table.

Using the full-size patterns in the instructions, cut the letters from scraps of 1x8-inch pine. And for year-round use, see pages 38 and 39 for a way to turn these same letters into an appealing gift for a special youngster.

A CHRISTMAS CELEBRATION

For a stellar Christmas celebration, these table decorations set a dazzling mood. Eight stars, assembled onto a 9-inch-square wooden frame, encircle the centerpiece, *below.* The stacked star candle holders complete the arrangement.

Cut out the stars using the full-size patterns, and purchase the candle cups at your crafts or lumber store.

Minature toys and tiny packages lie beneath the super-simple star tree, *opposite.* Little ones especially will enjoy this playful decoration.

Eleven stars, cut in ⅛-inch increments, form the boughs of the tree. Stack them atop a circular base with a dowel placed through the center. Top the stack with one more glorious star.

Paint the stars green, as shown in the photo, for an old-fashioned look. Or, sand them and wax for a natural finish that will fit in a contemporary setting.

Partridge in a Pear Tree Christmas Accent

Shown on page 56.

Finished size is approximately 16½ inches in diameter.

MATERIALS
15-inch square of ¾-inch plywood for the base
Scraps of ¼-inch hardboard for the pears, partridge, and nest
18 feet of ¼x1⅛-inch clear pine lath
Grape vine twigs for nest
Dark green, kelly green, yellow, red, gold, gray, and brown acrylic paints
Clear spray varnish
Carpenter's glue
Twenty-four ⅜-inch staples

INSTRUCTIONS
Center and draw a 13-inch-diameter base circle onto the ¾-inch plywood. Using the drawing, *opposite,* draw the 3¼-inch-wide extensions along the center top and bottom edges and ¾ inch beyond the circle. Cut the base circle, with its top and bottom knobs, from the plywood.

If you can't find ¼ × 1⅛-inch clear pine lath, cut wider lath to this width. Bevel the edges of the lath lightly with medium-grade sandpaper on a sanding block. Then cut the lath into 26 pieces, *each* 8½ inches long. Cut a 70-degree angle in one end of each lath piece.

Cut the squares from the waste of the lath pieces *after* you assemble and trim them on the plywood circle; instructions follow below.

Transfer the full-size patterns for the pears, partridge, and nest, on page 65, to ⅛-inch hardboard and cut these pieces out with a saber saw. Paint the top and sides of pears yellow; add gold highlights. Paint the stems and leaves dark green with brown veins on leaves. Paint the partridge with shades of browns and grays; use gold to highlight wing, breast, and tail feathers. Paint the ribbon gold, the holly kelly green, and the berries red.

To begin assembly, draw a line on the plywood base from the center points of the top and bottom knobs. Position two of the 8-inch lath pieces together at the 70-degree angle with their joint lining up directly on this line and with the point just touching the bottom of the knob. Attach these pieces with glue, but use it sparingly. Continue adding lath until you get to within three pieces of the top. Turn the workpiece over on a perfectly flat surface and place a heavy weight on the plywood. Let the glue dry.

Find the center of the lath sections by drilling a tiny hole up through the center point of the plywood circle. From this point, scribe a 15-inch-diameter circle atop the lath sections and cut the circle with a saber saw. Now that your circle is clearly defined, add the top pieces and trim as required. Paint the top and side edges dark green.

For the border trim, cut twenty-four 1⅛-inch squares from the leftover lath. Paint the top and sides of these pieces kelly green. Attach them to the back of the lath circle with ⅜-inch staples and glue.

Begin to fasten the squares at the center atop the notched edge. Trim away one corner of two squares; fasten one square to the left of the center and the other to the right of the center. Fasten the remaining squares (11 on each side), to the back of the lath circle. Position the squares so that one corner touches the plywood base and the side corners touch each other.

Note: It is not necessary to fasten the squares along the bottom of the circle, since the nest covers this portion.

Glue twigs to the nest piece to resemble a nest. Using the photo, page 56, as a guide, glue pears, nest, and partridge to the wreath. Spray entire piece with varnish.

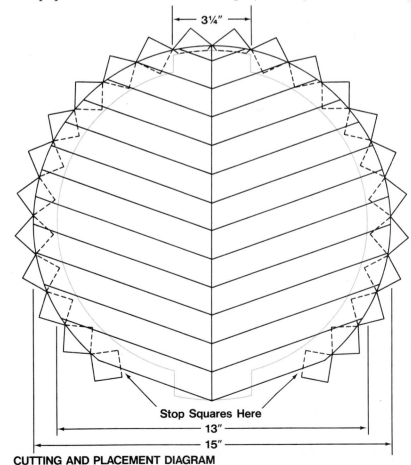

← 3¼" →

Stop Squares Here
← 13" →
← 15" →

CUTTING AND PLACEMENT DIAGRAM

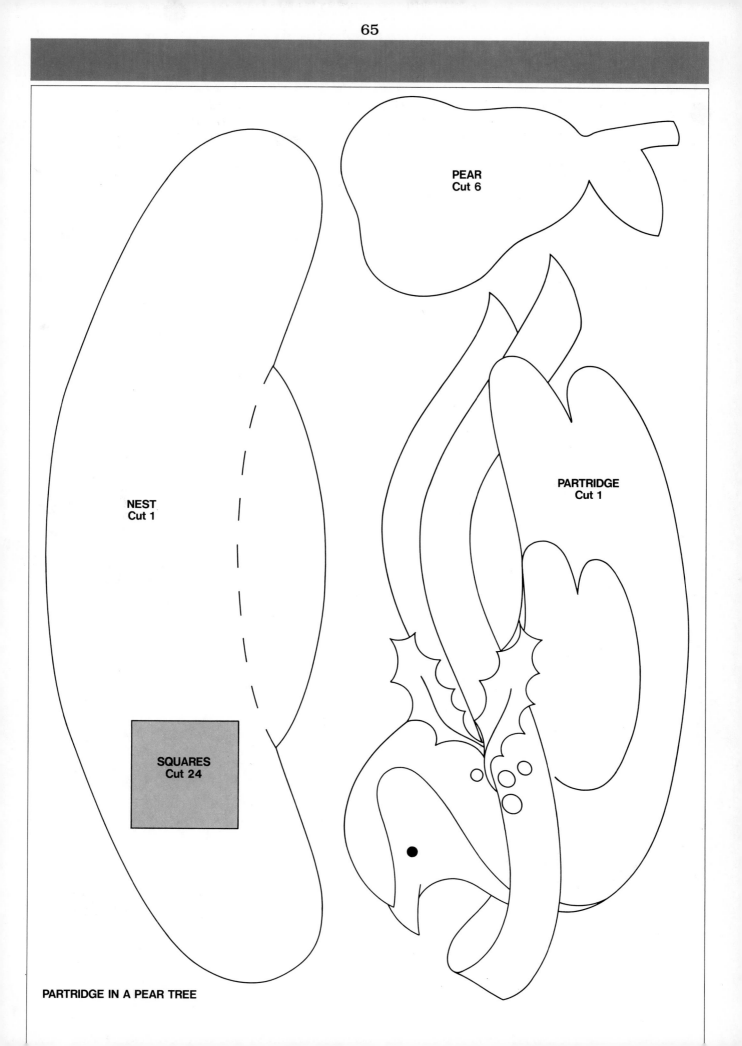

PEAR
Cut 6

NEST
Cut 1

PARTRIDGE
Cut 1

SQUARES
Cut 24

PARTRIDGE IN A PEAR TREE

A CHRISTMAS CELEBRATION

Woodburned Crèche

Shown on pages 58–59.

Figures vary in size; the arch stands 10½ inches tall.

MATERIALS
Scraps of ¼-inch fir plywood
Scraps of ¼-inch hardboard
Woodburning tool (available at lumber or crafts supply stores or by writing to Hot Tools, Inc., P.O. Box 615, Marblehead, MA 01945)
Acrylic paints in colors of your choice for the painted crèche
Walnut, cherry, and fruitwood stains for the stained crèche
Hot glue gun

INSTRUCTIONS
Trace the full-size patterns, *below* and on pages 67-69, onto tracing paper. Then transfer the patterns onto plywood. Cut out the figures.

Before you begin to woodburn the crèche figures, practice burning on scraps of the plywood so you know what to expect from the tips on your own tool and how much pressure to apply as you work to achieve the result you want. The plywood we used in our two crèche sets was very soft and little pressure was needed to define the lines.

When you are familiar with the tool and the wood you are working with, proceed to woodburn the outlines and all the details of the figures. For added interest, burn out some of the open areas of the pieces (see photographs on pages 58 and 59).

For the stained set, use different colors of stains to paint the clothing and other details. Use watered-down acrylics to paint the painted set.

Cut triangular standing bases to fit the backs of the pieces from the hardboard. The full-size pattern, *below,* fits the back of the sheep and the manger. Cut 2 bases for *each* of the sheep, donkey, and the arch. Adjust this pattern across the base and height to fit the taller pieces to prevent tipping over. Glue bases to back of figures with glue gun. Glue two bases to the legs of sheep, donkey, and arch.

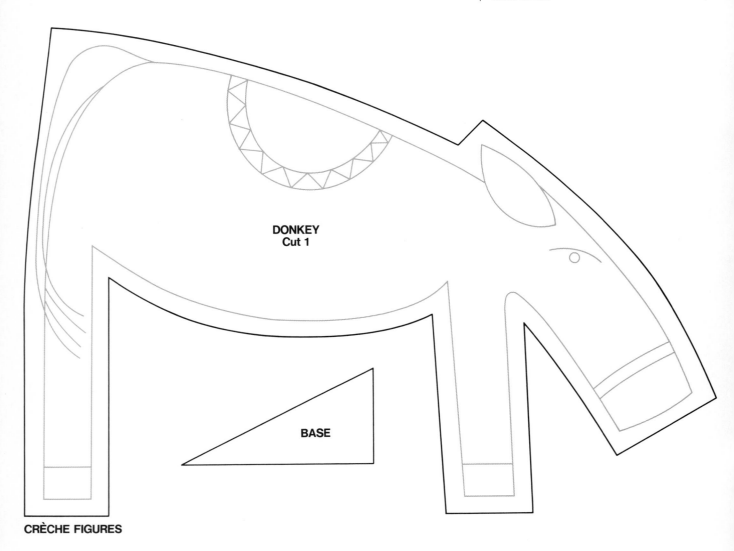

DONKEY
Cut 1

BASE

CRÈCHE FIGURES

Fold

5"

ARCH FOR CRÈCHE FIGURES

Woodburning Tips

Woodburning is easy and fun. With a little practice, you'll discover effective ways to work with a woodburning tool and with the types of wood that are best for successful woodburning projects. Here are some helpful hints to get you started with our woodburned project and any others that you might pursue.

Soft, even-grained woods, especially basswood, work best for woodburning. They burn quickly and their light color contrasts nicely with woodburning lines.

To transfer patterns to wood, use graphite paper with an ink pen or stylus. To avoid denting the wood, use minimal pressure to trace the pattern. Carbon paper and ink leave permanent markings on the wood that cannot be removed. If you miss a traced line when woodburning, a pencil eraser will easily remove graphite markings.

As you begin to work with the tool, hold it lightly and take your time. Practice on scrap pieces of the wood that you are going to work with before you begin the actual project.

Hold the tool as you hold a pencil. As you work, move the tool toward yourself. Hold the wood with the left hand (or with the right hand if you're left-handed) to help keep your work steady. Move the wood as you work to keep the tool in the correct position for burning.

Clean the carbon buildup from the tip of the tool every couple of hours. Simply slide the hot tool gently across fine sandpaper.

When all burning is complete, remove unburned tracing lines with a pencil eraser. Apply a clear sealant to the wood and lightly sand the surface.

You can also use oil-base pencils (pastels) to apply coloring to woodburned projects; these allow for shading and blending of colors. To prevent the colors from smearing after they are all applied, seal the wood with up to 3 coats of wood sealer. Sand, and apply more sealer to obtain a smooth surface.

A CHRISTMAS CELEBRATION

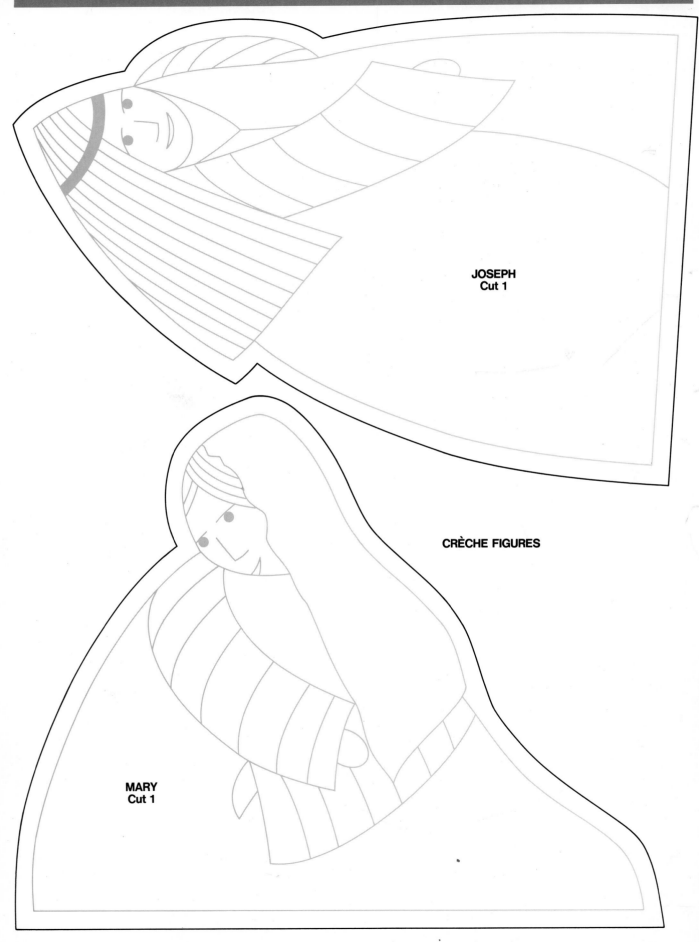

JOSEPH
Cut 1

CRÈCHE FIGURES

MARY
Cut 1

Snowman Tree Ornament

Shown on pages 60–61.

Snowman stands 4½ inches tall.

MATERIALS
Scraps of ¼-inch hardboard
White, black, green, and red
   acrylic paints
Small twig branches
Crafts glue
6-inch piece of ⅜-inch-wide
   plaid ribbon
Gold cord

INSTRUCTIONS
Following the heavy black line, trace the full-size pattern for the snowman, *below, right,* onto tracing paper; then transfer the pattern onto the hardboard. Cut the snowman from the wood. Sand all the side edges smooth.

With a ⁵⁄₆₄-inch drill bit, drill a hole in the top of the hat to hold the hanging cord. For placement of twig arms, drill two ¼-inch-deep holes into the sides of the snowman, following the direction of the dashed lines on the pattern.

Paint the front, sides, and back of hat black. Paint the front, sides and back of the snowman white. Then add facial details, hat trim, and buttons. Refer to photograph on pages 60 and 61 as a painting guide.

When dry, tie the plaid ribbon around the neck for a scarf. Glue down one end of the ribbon to his front. Glue small twigs into the side holes for his arms. Thread gold cord through top of his hat and knot to hang ornament.

SHEEP
Cut 2

INFANT
Cut 1

SNOWMAN TREE ORNAMENT

CRÈCHE FIGURES

A CHRISTMAS CELEBRATION

NOEL Letters

Shown on pages 60–61.

Tallest letter is 10¾ inches; all others are 7¾ inches.

MATERIALS
3½-foot piece of 1x8-inch pine
Carbon and tracing papers
Watercolor paintbrushes
Primer; clear spray varnish
Acrylic paints in the following
    colors: red, green, light rust,
    white, blue, pink, yellow, gray,
    and dark brown

INSTRUCTIONS
Trace the full-size letters on pages 72–75 onto tracing paper. The bear that sits atop the letter "E" is on page 75. Align the dashed lines on the two drawings to complete the pattern. Using carbon paper, trace the patterns onto the wood; cut out the letter shapes. Drill a hole in the waste area inside the letter "O" and insert the blade of the saw into the hole; cut out the inside area.

Lightly sand all edges. Then prime all surfaces.

Paint the back and sides of each letter red. Using the photograph on pages 60 and 61 as a guide, paint the details on the front side of each letter. Allow each color to completely dry before beginning the next color. For greater color intensity, add a second coat. To protect the painted surfaces, spray with varnish.

Star Tree Centerpiece

Shown on page 63.

Tree stands 12 inches high.

MATERIALS
5 foot length of 1x10-inch fir
10-inch length of ⅜-inch-
    diameter dowel
Paint primer
Red, green, and yellow acrylic
    paints
Satin varnish
Carpenter's glue

INSTRUCTIONS
Trace the small star pattern on page 71 on to tracing paper. Then enlarge this pattern in ⅛-inch increments to make 6 more star patterns. Then decrease the star pattern in ⅛-inch increments to make 4 more patterns. Trace patterns onto wood.

From fir, cut out 2 stars from the smallest pattern and 1 from each of the remaining star patterns. Cut one 4-inch-diameter circle for tree base.

With ⅜-inch drill bit, drill holes through center of 11 stars (do not drill a hole through the center of 1 of the smallest stars) and through center of the tree base. Drill 1-inch-deep hole between legs of 2 star points of remaining small star for tree top. Sand and prime all pieces (tops, bottoms, and sides).

Glue dowel into center of base; check to be sure it is perpendicular to the base. Allow this assembly to dry completely.

With red, paint base of tree; with yellow, paint star tree top; with green, paint remaining stars and dowel. When dry, coat all pieces with varnish.

Stack 11 green stars onto the dowel in order of size from largest to the smallest; top with the yellow star.

Star Candlesticks

Shown on page 62.

Candlesticks stand 3 inches high.

MATERIALS
2 feet of 1x10-inch fir for 2
    candlesticks
Two wood candle cups
Wood primer
Red and green acrylic paints
Carpenter's glue
Polyurethane satin varnish
Antique glazing
Two 1-inch No. 7 wood screws

INSTRUCTIONS
Trace large and small star patterns on page 71 onto tracing paper. For two candlesticks, trace two large stars and two small stars onto wood. Cut out shapes. Sand and prime all pieces. Paint tops and sides of the large stars green; paint tops and sides of small stars and candle cups red. When dry, coat with varnish.

Center and glue small star atop large star. Center and glue candle cup atop small star. For added strength, set screw through candle cup base. (Cups come with a countersink and shank hole in the bottom for a No. 7 screw.) To complete, apply antique glazing with a soft cloth, following the manufacturer's instructions.

Star Centerpiece

Shown on page 62.

Finished size of centerpiece is 13x13 inches; it stands approximately 4 inches tall.

MATERIALS
5 foot length of 1x6-inch fir
Four candle cups
Wood primer
Red and green acrylic paints
Carpenter's glue
Satin varnish
Antique glazing
Eight 5d finishing nails
Four 4d finishing nails
Eight 1½-inch No. 7 screws

INSTRUCTIONS
FOR THE STARS: From fir, cut 9 stars using the small star pattern on page 71. Set 8 aside. From the remaining star, cut 4 standing posts (supports) for the 4 stars that sit in center of sides, using the dashed lines on small star pattern; discard remains of star. Sand and prime all pieces and the 4 candle cups. Paint the stars red; paint the candle cups and standing posts green.

FOR THE BASE: Cut ¾-inch-square strips from scrap piece of ¾-inch fir. Miter the strips to 9 inches for outside length. Join the strips to form a frame. Use glue and 4d finishing nails. Once you have joined all sides, check to

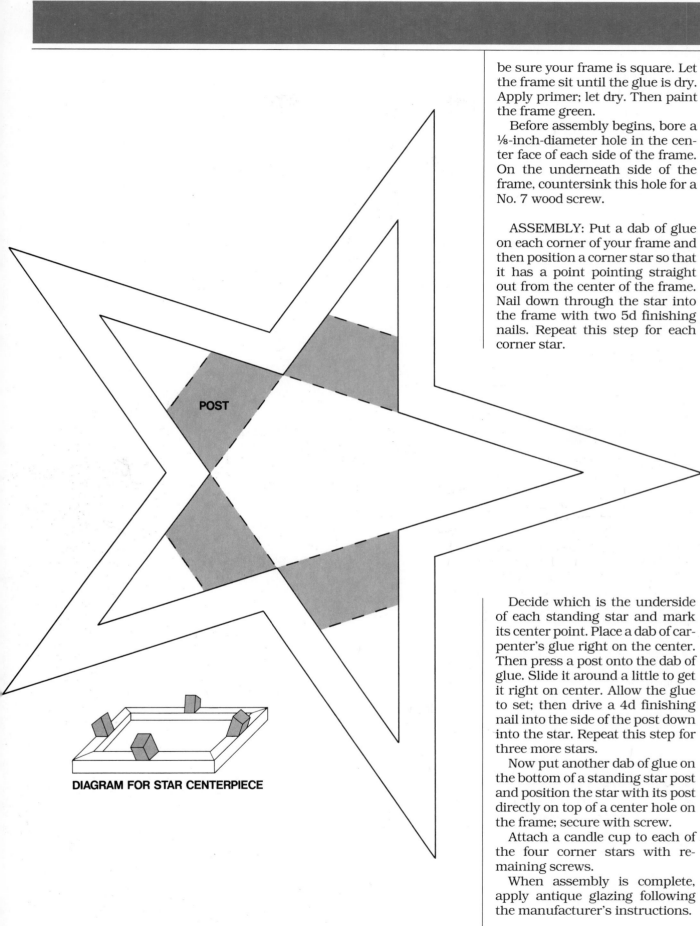

POST

DIAGRAM FOR STAR CENTERPIECE

STAR PATTERNS

be sure your frame is square. Let the frame sit until the glue is dry. Apply primer; let dry. Then paint the frame green.

Before assembly begins, bore a ⅛-inch-diameter hole in the center face of each side of the frame. On the underneath side of the frame, countersink this hole for a No. 7 wood screw.

ASSEMBLY: Put a dab of glue on each corner of your frame and then position a corner star so that it has a point pointing straight out from the center of the frame. Nail down through the star into the frame with two 5d finishing nails. Repeat this step for each corner star.

Decide which is the underside of each standing star and mark its center point. Place a dab of carpenter's glue right on the center. Then press a post onto the dab of glue. Slide it around a little to get it right on center. Allow the glue to set; then drive a 4d finishing nail into the side of the post down into the star. Repeat this step for three more stars.

Now put another dab of glue on the bottom of a standing star post and position the star with its post directly on top of a center hole on the frame; secure with screw.

Attach a candle cup to each of the four corner stars with remaining screws.

When assembly is complete, apply antique glazing following the manufacturer's instructions.

A CHRISTMAS CELEBRATION

NOEL LETTERS

A CHRISTMAS CELEBRATION

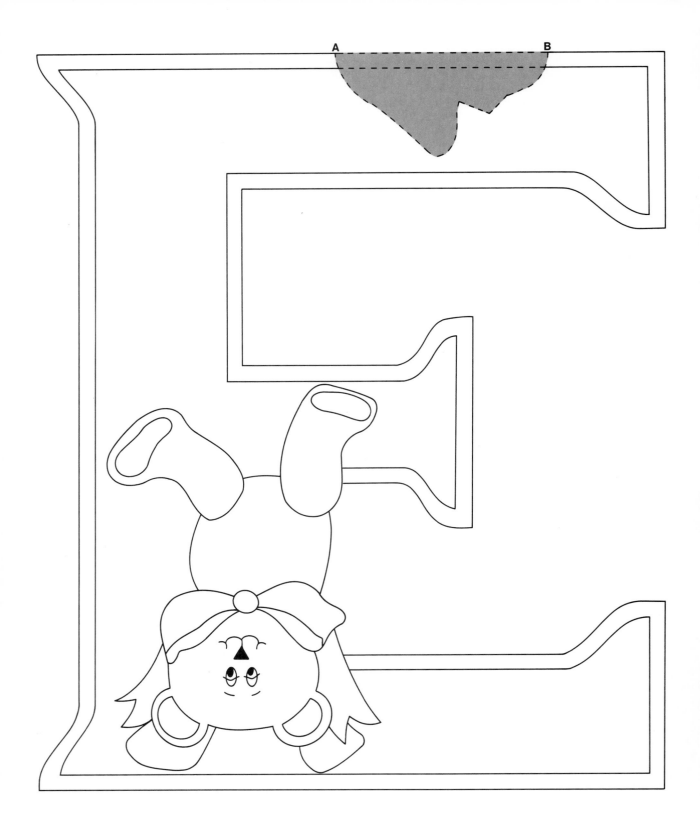

WOODWORKING PRIMER

From just a scrap of wood, a woodcrafter can create practical things and wonderful toys and accessories for gift giving, bazaars, and niches throughout the home.

To help you pursue your wood crafting endeavors, here and on the next two pages are tips for tools, fasteners, and finishing techniques. Additional information on lumber and other wood materials can be found on page 55.

Tools of the Trade

You can create a surprising number of woodworking projects with a minimum number of tools. Experienced woodworkers, however, know how satisfying it is to have the right tool for the right job. The ideal beginning woodcrafter's tool box contains the 17 pieces noted below (listed in order of importance). Tools at the top of the list are used most often by woodworkers. If you see an item that's higher in the list than you would expect, that's because you won't find a good substitute for that particular tool.

BASIC WOODWORKER'S
TOOL BOX
1. rule
2. square
3. saw
4. hammer
5. power drill
6. screwdriver
7. pliers
8. wrench
9. plane
10. chisel
11. rasp
12. sanding block
13. awl
14. putty knife
15. utility knife
16. clamp
17. miter box

If you are just beginning to collect tools, first buy those that are at the top of the list and work your way down. Because a tool is usually a lifetime investment, it pays to spend a few dollars more and get the best quality tool available. The highest price, however, doesn't always guarantee the best quality. To help you recognize top-grade equipment, we've included shopping tips in our discussion of types of tools, *below*.

It's a good idea to think of tools by function. This keeps you mindful of your options when selecting tools for each phase of your project. The tools we have gathered for our basic tool box fall into eight main groups. These groups are: (1) measuring, (2) laying-out and marking, (3) cutting, (4) shaping, (5) driving, (6) joining, (7) finishing tools, and (8) multi-function tools.

MEASURING TOOLS: Measuring tools are usually the first ones you reach for when you begin a project. A *6-foot folding wood rule* is the most common and convenient to use. Check the action on a folding rule. It should fold and unfold easily. Don't expect one that is stiff to loosen with use.

If your materials or projects are large, you might also consider a *16-foot steel tape measure*. Buy a tape measure that is at least ¾ inch wide and one that has a "friction tooth" or grid on the end tab. This helps hold the tab when you need to hook it over an edge. Your tape should have a lock for locking the tape out at any point. Avoid pressing the rewind button; winding back the tape at full speed eventually will pull the end tab off.

LAYING-OUT TOOLS: Laying out is the process of measuring and marking the cutting lines for a project. You can use a wood or steel rule, but sooner or later you will need a *framing square* for laying out and checking right angles. Framing squares are either steel or aluminum.

Right-angle cutting lines are also marked on planks or boards with a *combination square* or a *try square*. These two tools are also used to check the accuracy of your cuts.

When shopping for a combination or try square, buy one that has a bracket that can be tightened against the rule, and reads square when it's tight. There's no need to pay extra for one that contains a scribing needle and a bubble level.

Keep a compass, some pencils, and a hand-held pencil sharpener in your box, too.

CUTTING TOOLS: Start your saw collection with a *10-point cross-cut handsaw* with a 24- or 26-inch blade. The point size tells you how many teeth the saw has per inch—the greater the number of points, the finer the cut. "Cross-cut" means the points are staggered to enhance cutting action. This easy-to-handle saw produces a relatively clean-cut edge.

Fine cuts are made with a *dovetail saw*. Irregular and interior cuts are made with a *coping saw*.

Handsaw blades of American and Swedish steel are the best quality and the most expensive. Top-grade steel blade are worth the cost.

Support your investment in expensive tools by taking good care of them. Protect the blades of all your saws when they are not in use.

Once you become experienced with handsaws, consider buying a power saw. For craft projects, a *saber saw* is useful, but even the best saber saw does not make perfectly vertical cuts. In other words, saber saws are not precision instruments. Pay only what is necessary to buy one that includes a splinter guard.

For lots of heavy ripping (cutting wood along the grain) of either sheet goods or solid wood and cross-cutting (cutting across the grain), purchase a *circular saw* that uses a 7-inch-diameter blade. Ask to plug in a circular saw before you buy it; make sure its sound does not hurt your ears.

A drill is a specialized cutting tool that cuts or, more properly, bores holes. Buy an *electric drill* with a ⅜-inch chuck and a 12- to 16-piece set of brad-point bits, ranging in size from ⅟₁₆ to ¼-inch. You needn't pay a lot for a power drill; pass up the fancy variable speed for a cordless two-speed plastic-case model.

SHAPING TOOLS: These tools are handy after cutting tools have done the major work. A *low-angle block plane* is the most useful and adaptable shaping tool. This plane smooths and rounds rough edges. The blade requires good care and must be kept sharp. Always store your plane on its side, never right-side-up.

A *wood rasp* looks like a file, but there's a difference between a real file, which is for metal work, and a rasp. The most commonly used wood rasp is called a *bastard 8-inch half-round*. Use this tool to further smooth the edges that you rounded with the block plane. You'll find a *6-inch rattail rasp* a handy tool for trimming up the insides of small holes and contours. Rasps have a squared projection at one end for mounting in a handle. If you find yourself using these tools frequently, buy handles for them. It's no fun rasping the skin off your hand.

Chisels are sometimes considered tools for advanced woodworkers. They're also wonderful tools for beginners to use, and it's not hard to learn how to use them. Buy a set of four chisels ranging ¼- to 1-inch size. Keep them sharp and learn to care for them properly. Buy steel chisels with steel butt handles. Plastic handles with plastic butts will eventually wear out or become misshapen, rendering the chisel useless.

DRIVING TOOLS: Two of the most common kinds of *screw drivers* are *flat-head* and *Phillips*. Buy one of each kind that will fit screw sizes 6 through 8.

Hammers, too, are driving tools. You can't go wrong with a 13-ounce curve claw hammer with a wooden handle. For brads and tacks, use a tack hammer. Keep a ⅟₃₂-point-size nail set close to your hammer for setting nails. A wood handle is the only kind you'll want on your hammer. Fiber and metal handles don't absorb shock as well as wood handles do.

JOINING TOOLS: These tools are better known as *clamps*. They're used to hold glued parts together under pressure while the glue dries. They can also be helpful for holding work pieces upright or in a certain position while you are working on them. There are many different kinds and many different sizes of each kind. C-clamps are for small jobs; bar and pipe clamps for large jobs. Wait to buy clamps in the sizes you need as your projects require. In no time at all, you'll develop a selection that's just right for you.

Pipe clamps are the best buy in clamps because you supply the pipe yourself. Also, you can take the fittings off any particular length of pipe and use them on another length.

FINISHING TOOLS: *Sandpaper* is the most common finishing tool. Refer to page 36 for some tips on the different grades of paper and their uses.

When buying *paint brushes,* remember that good quality nylon or polyester-bristle brushes are well worth the money when applying the final coat of latex paint. The price of brushes is not determined by the type of bristle, but by the way the bristles are set in the brush. You don't want them constantly pulling loose and ending up on the painted surface. Brushes come in various sizes. A collection of three, ranging in sizes from ½ inch to 1½ inches, will see you through most jobs.

Foam brushes are also handy for working on small projects.

A *putty knife* can be considered a woodworker's finishing tool. Use it to fill nail holes and countersunk screw holes with wood putty. It's also used to shave a filled hole smooth before sanding.

Pay a little more for a chrome or stainless steel putty knife. Putty knives are often used with water-base compounds, and rust can be a problem with a steel knife.

MULTI-FUNCTION TOOLS: These tools do not fit nicely into the above types grouped by function because they can do many jobs. For this reason it is hard to get along without them, and they are just as important as tools that have a single function.

Pliers are the most familiar tool in this group. Probably, you already have regular 8-inch pliers or a plumber's wrench in the house. You will find many uses for these tools in woodworking projects too. Buy a set of needle-nose pliers, too.

When you have goofed driving a finishing nail or brad, bending the nail down close to the surface in a single blow, use *6-inch end cutters* or *end nippers* to cut the head off the nail. Set what's left of the nail and fill the hole. This is much easier than pulling the nail out and poses less risk of damaging the surface of your project.

Use an *8-inch adjustable-end wrench* for tightening nuts and for other jobs throughout the house.

An *awl* is used to start small holes for screws or to locate the exact position in which you want to bore a hole with a drill and bit.

A *utility knife* might be classified with the cutting tools or with the marking tools. Its razor-sharp blade is great for small cutting or trimming jobs. The blade is often used to scribe a very fine cutting line, so it's also a marking tool. However you wish to use it, choose the kind with a retractable blade. It's the safest.

continued

WOODWORKING PRIMER

A *miter box* is used in combination with a *backsaw* to cut miters; the 45-degree angle cuts that form square corners when joined. Buy an ordinary maple miter box and backsaw. This miter box delivers as much precision as other boxes that are more expensive.

Building a work bench is the first step in staking out a certain area of the basement or garage as your own shop. After you've built yours, install a *bench vise*, which is like a stationary clamp.

Fasteners

Steel nails are the most common wood fasteners. There are many kinds of steel nails, but the beginning woodworker needs just a few kinds. Learning to choose the right nail for the job is easy.

The most common nails the woodworker uses are finishing nails in sizes from 2d to 8d. The small "d" is the designation for the "penny system" of measuring nail length. (In a hardware store, you'll ask for "two-penny nails." In writing, they'll be designated as "2d nails.")

Here's how the penny system works: The smallest nail, the 2d nail, is 1 inch long. The number sizes increase by one for every ¼-inch increase in length—all the way up to 60d for 6 inches. The diameter or gauge of the nail also increases as the nails get longer, but the range is very small for finishing nails and you do not need to be concerned with gauge size. The common sizes of finishing nails a woodworker uses are listed below:

NAIL LENGTH BY THE
PENNY SYSTEM
2d = 1″
3d = 1¼″
4d = 1½″
5d = 1¾″
6d = 2″
7d = 2¼″
8d = 2½″

Brads are the other kind of nails used most often by woodworkers. Generally, brads are smaller than finishing nails in gauge size and may be from ½ to 1½ inches long.

Brads are not classified by the penny system. Choose nails or brads at least three times as long as the width of the wood you are driving them through. For example, use a ¾-inch-long brad to nail a ¼-inch-thick piece of wood to a 1-inch-thick piece. Use the chart below as a guide:

CHOOSING NAIL SIZE
Use 3d or 4d finishing nails for
⅜″ thick wood
Use 4d or 5d finishing nails for
½″ thick wood
Use 5d or 6d finishing nails for
⅝″ thick wood
Use 6d to 8d finishing nails for
¾″ thick wood

NAILING TECHNIQUES
Most woodworking requires that you nail through the flat side of a board or piece of plywood into the edge of an abutting piece. Position the nail so it will penetrate into the center of the edge. Otherwise, drive nails about ¾ inch from any edge. Tap the nail a few times to get it started, and then, using forearm action, strike the nail squarely on the head as you drive it down flush with the surface. Never strike the nail beyond this point with the hammer head.

When the nail is flush, set it below the surface with a nail set. Place the point of the set squarely on top of the nail head and tap the nail-set head a couple times.

When you are doing a lot of nailing, you will want to drive all nails flush first and then go back and set them. To get brads started, hold them lightly with needle-nose pliers or a brad pusher.

Sometimes, depending on the composition and moisture content of your material, you may have trouble with nails splitting the wood. The nails are acting as wedges as they are driven into the wood and this forces surrounding wood fiber outward.

To prevent splitting, blunt the nail points slightly before you drive them. Place the nail head against a solid surface and just tap the point once or twice. A blunt point causes the wood fibers to break and become compacted at the point around the nail.

Bore a pilot hole in hardwood before nailing. (Many hardwoods are so dense that you can't drive a nail without a pilot hole.)

A handy way to bore a hole is to nip the head off a smaller size finishing nail and place it in your drill. The wedge-shape point of the nail forces and compacts wood fiber to the side of the pilot hole as it twists into the wood. This gives extra holding power to the nail.

SCREWS: Like nails, there are many kinds of screws available in many sizes. Woodworkers mostly use *straight-slot, flathead wood screws* in lengths from ½ to 2 inches. The measuring system for screws is a little more complicated than the system for nails, because screws have different diameters or gauges, depending on the length of the screw.

The material you're using determines the size screw you need. Consider the thickness of the two pieces of wood or plywood that you are screwing together, and then choose a length that will allow two-thirds of the screw to penetrate into the second piece. Generally, the smallest gauge available in that length is the best. If you think you need extra holding power or if you're working with heavy materials like ¾-inch plywood, choose a larger gauge in that same length. The information below will help you choose the correct screw size for a certain thickness of wood.

CHOOSING SCREW SIZES
¼-inch plywood, use a ¾-inch
screw, No. 4 gauge
⅜-inch plywood, use a 1-inch
screw, No. 6 gauge
½-inch plywood, use a 1¼-inch
screw, No. 6 gauge
⅝-inch plywood, use a 1¼-inch
screw, No. 8 gauge
¾-inch plywood or fir, use a
1½-inch screw, No. 8 gauge

An *awl* is often used to make a starting hole for short, small-gauge screws when you are working in softwoods like fir or pine. Just push the point in with hand force or give the awl handle a thump with the ball in the palm of your hand. Move the awl around once or twice. This produces a pilot hole and a countersink at the same time.

A drill bit that's slightly smaller than the screw root may be used to bore pilot holes for larger screws in soft wood. Drill a hole partway through your top piece to accommodate the screw shank. This is called a a shank hole. Then, drill a deeper pilot hole (no deeper than the length of the screw) for the screw threads, using a bit with a smaller diameter. Finally, use a countersink bit to make a shallow depression at the top of the shank hole area. Check that the countersink is wide enough for the head of the screw.

Place the screw in position and begin driving with a screw driver properly matched to the screw head. If a lot of resistance develops as soon as the shank of your screw enters the wood, your shank hole is not wide enough.

Hardwood pilot holes always require the three-step pilot hole as described above.

Countersinking screws is similar to setting nails. You countersink so that the head of the screw is flush with the surface. Also, you can sink the head well below the surface and fill the hole with wood putty, commercial wood plugs, or decorative buttons.

GLUES: Also called carpenter's glue, wood glue is a polyvinyl-acetate resin emulsion. White, or sometimes tan, it dries almost clear. It is water-soluble until it dries, when it becomes water-resistant.

There is one basic rule to using glue: Use only enough. Too much glue causes lots of glue to squeeze out of joints. This glue squeeze-out must be cleaned up. Even though the glue is water-soluble, you shouldn't have to clean it off unfinished wood. Avoid the problem by learning how much is just

enough. It's okay to have a few beads collecting along the glued edge.

Run a bead of glue over both surfaces to be joined and then spread the glue with a flat stick or your finger. Place the pieces together. Slide them back and forth against one another just a little ways once or twice. Remember, oozing glue means you are using too much. Sand the beads off the edges after the glue is completely dry.

Use glue in combination with nails or screws for extra-strong joints. When using nails, set your nails before you apply glue.

Clamps are handy tools to use when gluing. Use them to stabilize glued pieces while you drive nails or screws.

If you are using just glue, without nails or screws, clamps should be left on for 24 hours.

Finishing Techniques

Finishing is a part of woodworking that is just as important as building the project itself. The finish often highlights the project's design while preserving and protecting the wood. The three most common kinds of finishes used by woodworkers are paint, stain, and varnish.

PAINT: Latex paint is available in matte and semi-gloss finishes. It has been refined and developed to such an extent that it rivals the old oil-base enamels in durability and colorfastness. Because it is soluble in water, it is safer to use, and spills can be cleaned up with relatively little trouble. For these reasons, latex paint has almost replaced oil-base enamels in the woodworker's shop.

Preparation of the surface is the key to a good paint job. The surface should be as smooth as the base material allows. This means sanding with heavy and medium sandpaper if necessary and then, for soft wood surfaces, final-sanding a third time with fine paper.

Further smoothing with steel wool is often recommended for hardwoods.

Remove all sanding dust by wiping with a tack cloth. Buy a tack cloth at the hardware store or make your own as follows: Boil 3 tablespoons of lemon oil in a quart of water. Saturate clean cotton cloths with this mixture. Wring out excess water and hang cloths to dry. Store cloths in plastic bags.

The next step after sanding is to apply a primer, which acts as both a sealer and a filler. Ask your paint dealer for advice on the best product available for the material you are using. Don't skip the priming step. Most wood surfaces cannot alone provide a good base for paint.

Apply paint in even coats with even strokes back and forth until the surface is uniformly covered. Do not continue brushing over the same area for more than three or four passes. Feather out the brush strokes as you work.

Always clean your brushes immediately after use. Wash them in tepid clear water. Shake out rinse water. Shape the bristles into a wedge while they are still wet, and allow the brushes to dry.

STAINS: There are water-base stains and oil-base stains in many colors and shades. Most stains are colored to complement natural wood colors. Penetrating oil-base stains are more popular and easier to apply than water-base stains. Apply these stains liberally with any kind of a brush. Allow the stain to set for about 20 minutes and wipe dry with a clean cloth, working in the direction of the grain.

VARNISH: Polyurethane is the pick of woodworkers today. It produces a tough, flexible finish that's very resistant to chipping and scratching. It's available in glass-clear high-gloss or semi-matte. If you are looking for a high-gloss finish, consider painting your project and then giving it a final coat with polyurethane. Check for compatibility with the color coat when buying varnish.

ACKNOWLEDGMENTS

Our special thanks to the following designers who contributed projects to this book.

Kathy Engel—4–5, 20, 40–41, 56–57

Sarah Grant-Hutchison—58–59

Eric Haldeman—6

Linda Hermanstorfer—24, 26–27

Joanne Hurley—21, 23

Michael Stowers—9, 44–45

Sara Jane Treinen—22, 25, 62–63

Bonnie Wedge—7, 39, 43, 60–61

Jim Williams—8, 38

We also are pleased to acknowledge the following photographers, whose talents and technical skills contributed much to this book.

Hopkins Associates—4–5, 6–7, 8–9, 21, 38–39, 40–41, 42–43, 44–45, 56–57

Mike Jensen—27

Perry Struse—20–21, 22–23, 24–25, 26, 58–59, 60–61, 62–63

For their technical skills and cooperation, we extend special thanks to:

Linda Emmerson

Ron Hawbaker

Stacey Molloy

Tom Thompson

Jack West

Don Wipperman

Chris Neubauer

For their cooperation and courtesy, we extend special thanks to the following source:

Hot Tools, Inc.,
P.O. Box 615
Marblehead, MA 01945

Have BETTER HOMES AND GARDENS® magazine delivered to your door. For information, write to: MR. ROBERT AUSTIN, P.O. BOX 4536, DES MOINES, IA 50336.